A dedication

This Book "Over the Hills" is dedicated to the eight young men who pioneered Green Mountains.

OVER THE HILLS

by

BERNARD O'REILLY

FORTITUDE PRESS

Third Impression 1974
National Library of Australia ISBN 0 85881 007 7

Introduction

This is a very untidy book—written without plot or plan; the reader need not look for continuity, there isn't any.

There is an attempt to see behind the intangible influences of Mountains—a futile attempt—but some things mentioned may strike a familiar chord with those who have a deep and enduring love for the everlasting hills.

BERNARD O'REILLY.

"Goblin Wood,"
  Green Mountains.

Mountains

OUNTAIN madness would seem to be inherent—it has been with me as long as conscious thought. It is too subtle for description or analysis; as easy to track down as the intricate pattern of perfume wisps from the jungle on warm, damp days; as fleeting and as unsubstantial as those flashes of familiar near-memory which arise almost to our consciousness and then dissolve for ever.

My boyhood home was surrounded by hills, rounded hills through which Long Swamp Creek wound a snaky course. Marsden's Rock, over whose shoulder the sun rose, was a scant mile away. Round Ridge, behind which it set, was only two hundred yards up from the cart shed. I seemed to live down in a crater shut in by rims beyond which were wonderful and inaccessible things, things that were farther away than the moon, for the moon, when it was big and round and yellow as butter, perched on the black rim of Marsden's Rock and actually seemed to be in Dad's back paddock.

In that small crater which was my world, the banked fires of my longings and imaginings smouldered and stirred uneasily—sometimes finding explosion in a sharp heart pain in the contemplation of a towering mushroom of thundercloud rosy with evening; sometimes, too, when I climbed to Redfern Hill on the south of the crater and looked away to the giant red cliffs of the Blue Mountains, whilst grand chords of unearthly music crashed through my mind. That music! It came up with me so naturally from babyhood that it has never seemed strange or out of place; through life it has been impossible to contemplate the grandeur of mountain or valley or to see the splendour of clouds fired by afterglow, without hearing the thunders of silent music. What was the melody? There wasn't one—there was nothing that the words of man could describe or that he could set to music on any stave—Wagner might have tried. What were the instruments? None that mind of man conceived nor the art of man could fashion or play, yet there they are and always have been. Explanation? Who knows? But it is a thought that, in the presence of things sublime, we draw so near to the Infinite that some of Its echoes come through to us. That, too, seems to be borne out by the hurt which the Sublime can give. The most beautiful scenes of my life—the ruby and gold of unforgettable sunsets, the majesty of storm-breeding mountains—were a joy to behold.

Theirs was a tormenting beauty which wrung out the heart; a mighty force which searched the soul. Why should this be? Why should not exquisite beauty bring exquisite joy instead of hurt? If there is an answer, it would seem to be that mortal men are so imperfect in themselves that perfection is too strong for them, just as bright sunshine is a dazzling, intolerable glare to the creatures of the night and dwellers in dark places.

There was a period in my life—a rather long period—when I turned my back on mountain sunsets and deliberately went indoors where I could not see them; it was a period of cowardice and running away of which I am not very proud, but it is being set down here to record the fact that one may fear exquisite beauty more than danger or ridicule.

It was the coming of school days which brought mountains more regularly into my life . . . the school track, as it meandered two miles upstream, rose and fell across ridges which gave views of Alum Mount, Minni Minni and the Divide. The Divide, high, grim and featureless, towered over the head of Long Swamp Creek—pale with summer haze, black under storm clouds, white with the winter snows or angry with bushfire, it was always the vast backdrop to our school journey.

The Great Divide dominated the scene, but its influence was subtle—insidiously it became part of the lives of the small people who trod the school track; they saw it as their farthest horizon and the loftiest terrestrial height to which they could lift their vision, but it was more than that; it was a lamp in the small street of their lives and, as with all street lights, its influence was mainly noticed when it was no longer there.

When, later in life, I lived for a time on the plains, my spirit was like a bird whose wings have been taken away; only the brief and splendid fires of dawn and dusk broke the flat, grey monotony of life. Just one mountain, ever so distant and blue, would have lit my drab world; it was then that the truth really came home—that a mountain was as necessary to my spirit as air was to my lungs.

But there were odd times in my schooldays when the mountain made demands on my consciousness—spring days when the Divide was sapphire blue against a while balloon of cloud and the breeze down the creek brought promise of wattle and honeysuckle—then, suddenly, the breath would shorten and a small heart twist with a hungry longing which was an acute physical hurt . . . longing for what? Nothing material; nothing that could be put in thought or word. Was it that the spirit, chastened by a beauty which excluded earthly things, was close beside the curtain of the Unknowable? Maybe disciples of Freud could find many explanations of these phenomena, but, for me, my thoughts on the matter satisfy without explaining. It is enough for me that a lovely flower is, without worrying why it is. If others wish to explain the inexplicable, they are welcome to try but let Science first solve the simple, everyday mystery of life before applying the micrometer and set square to the dawn mists of the Cosmos.

To me, it is a simple and a natural thing that religion and mountains have always been associated even in the most primitive cults; vaguely, with our imperfect minds, we glimpse a reflection of the Creator in those mighty monuments of the creation.

Minni Minni, Alum Mount and Table Rock— three peaks which abutted the Divide—wore crowns of marine sandstone, part of an ocean bed once a thousand fathoms deep, which the granite core of the Divide has pushed up four thousand feet above sea level, only to be etched away again by the rains of the ages and returned down the rivers to the sea once more, leaving but three fragments to tell of the timeless forces of the world. Some day in the far future, aeons after Minni Minni and her sisters have returned to the bosom of their mother ocean, the vast, silent and nameless machinery which works ceaselessly beneath our feet may lift them once again to the snows of a distant winter.

How many empires will wax and wane, how many dictators will force their will on the masses, how many noble cities will rise, crumble and blow away in dust before even a small segment of that giant cycle has been traced? Man the lord of creation? The conceited ant!

In the little, two by two, glass "museum" of the tiny Megalong Valley school, there was an irregular piece of brownish rock from Alum Mount; it rested on a shelf between a piece of petrified wood and a bottled brown snake and it was a conglomeration of fossilized sea shells and other marine life. To the small scholars, there was nothing nearly as unlikely in the Arabian Nights as the tale of lofty Alum Mount with its head thousands of feet below the blue, tossing ocean; in that, they showed the basic wisdom of children, for there is nothing that the imagination of man can conceive, be it ever so fantastic, which could be a fraction as extravagant as the story of the world. The human mind may accept the creation of another human mind because that is on its own plane, but it will grope in bewilderment before the mysteries of the creation—turning back on its own inventions in an effort to explain away that which it is too small to grasp.

In my tiny days, Mount Alum was the goblin which persistently haunted me: from several miles away, it leered with a giant, evil face, two heavy-lidded eyes which were shallow caverns in the ancient, rotten cliffs and the twisted scar of a landslide on its lower face. Perhaps, had I then known its history, I should have been even more afraid of this monster which had risen from the dark depths of the ocean. In the days when I saw it there were uneasiness and a feeling of evil which was vague and there was silent music, not the sonorous music of the sunsets, but uncanny music in minor key with no melody and less than an octave in range.

But it was at night, in the dark of my room, that the haunting really began. I saw its twisted face as the embodiment of all the evil bred of darkness. I could shut its image out of my eyes and its song out of my ears only by staring and concentrating upon the pale square of window—at times sleep gave me no refuge from the hated face, it followed me in nightmare.

After I outgrew this phase, the mountain still remained unfriendly and echoes of the weird, minor keys still persisted until, at the age of seven, I left the old home on Long Swamp. There came a day later in life when I was to hear that music, really hear it, with the ears instead of the mind. It was up in the Hebron Mountains of Palestine and it came from the crude reed pipes of Bedouin shepherd boys; with it came a feeling of loneliness, depression and the utter futility of life.

Hearth-stones and Memories

𝕿ABLE Rock was a friendly mountain capped by a great stone anvil for ever pointing northward—the first settlers had aptly named it Anvil Rock; a pity the name was lost for here was a fitting anvil for the forge of Vulcan.

At a small age, there was a solemn resolution to climb Table Rock some day—and I did, a quarter of a century later. I had returned from Queensland on a pilgrimage to the shrines of Long Swamp and so, one sharp blue morning in early Spring, I set out for the rock in the company of Pat, Alex and Will Cullen, three mates of the old Long Swamp School. There was something almost unnerving about the summit. The anvil top, roughly fifty yards by twenty, was devoid of plant or soil and perfectly flat, save for inch-deep pools of melted snow water; the walls fell away at ninety degrees from knife-sharp edges, so that, to one standing in the centre, the table was the whole world—the rest of the mountain and its surroundings were out of sight; behind the rim, there were distances blue and far away. I was riding alone on a tiny, flat planet. It was only by going to the rim and looking down on the roof of Grandfather's house and the friendly nearness of Long Swamp and its windings, that my world was restored. The view—there had been many in my life grander and more extensive—was an eagle's view of the land of my babyhood and boyhood—every roof top and rounded hill top, every dark, winding line of creek timber, every facet of the distant cliffs a memory; I was looking not only across the land but across the years.

The Rock had long been a magnet for climbers and I read the record of initials and dates cut in the soft sandstone. The fathers of our district had been there, men who had gone long before my time, but whose names I remembered so well. There were three young men—one of them my own brother, who had long been sleeping in France—but the list was incomplete; time and weather had erased many a name and that is why I looked in vain for the letters, "JANE M."; they had been carved on the Rock in 1880; that I knew, but the winds, the rains and the snows of seventy years had erased my mother's name.

Down at the foot of the walls, just before they give way to steep mountainside, are shallow caverns where the wallaroos shelter in rough weather. These caverns show large deposits of alum. From here, a spur takes a long running plunge to Grandfather's house in a creek bend amongst the willows; the house still stands and its large chimney of rough granite with local mud for plaster is the loveliest chimney I've ever seen. Even a Virginia creeper of Grandfather's day trails wine-red in autumn across the shaky veranda. Close by is the present Cullen homestead—it is a comforting thought that Grandfather's property has fallen into the gentle hands of our dear old neighbours and friends, the Cullens.

Half-a-mile upstream from the house, near where Paddy's Creek emerges from its little dark glen hung with drapes of clematis, is a sad and lonely hearth-stone, well-grown with green moss—all that a bushfire has left of an earlier home—that and some blue and white periwinkles, and some fragments of coloured china. I stood and listened to the tinkling of sheep bells far up the ridge and to the soft voice of Paddy's Creek, as it went among the boulders, to join Long Swamp, and I thought of that house on bitter nights with heavy snow on Table Rock; thought of the huge fire that roared on that hearth, and children's faces in the firelight, and the banter and the laughter, and I thought of Jane as a girl and wondered if her laughter often rang by that hearth. As a woman, Jane seldom laughed; often she smiled. Why is it that pilgrimages have to be sad? Why cannot places where people once laughed and were happy retain an aura of that happiness when the laughter has gone? But they never do. The words of a song came back and throbbed through my mind to the gentle lapping of Paddy's Creek—"Silent now is the wild and lonely glen, where the bright gay laughter echoes ne'er again."

Over on the far side of Long Swamp, in a clearing which still faintly showed the furrow marks of a plough long since rusted, stood the last of the fruit trees—a defiant, shaggy old hermit of a plum tree, innocent of a pruning knife these two generations, his unruly boughs and thickets of rods giving nesting sanctuary to several families of flame robins, whilst a whole swarm of bees droned in the great, white cumulus cloud of his blossom.

A mile away, up in a pocket by Blackfellow's Hill, there was another mute hearth-stone; there were willows in the gully and a wild hedge of blackberry and nearby was a thicket of cherry trees; some were the original trees planted long ago, the others were suckers and seedlings, but all were fruitful. England's home had once been there and it was Granny England, dead long before my time, who had walked and carried the young trees on her back from Mount Victoria on the Blue Mountains, fifteen miles away. But of generations of children who gorged themselves there each summer, few would have remembered or even thought to ask about the origin of the trees; they spoke of "England's where the cherries are" the same as they'd speak of "Mail box where the letters are." "England" was an impersonal someone who supplied cherries for a brief season of the year.

Browsing around England's with only my thoughts for company, I found broken pieces of blue and white china and then, where recent rains had uncovered it, part of an old, red, powder flask, the kind that went with the muzzle-loaders and the wallaby drives and the brumby-running, and those grand, galloping days of the last century. Those scraps of china are still with me somewhere on a shelf with fragments of marble and pottery from the ruins of Ascalon, a little stone axe from New Guinea, some seashells from Borneo and other odd things I've picked up in odd places. I wonder did the bower birds learn from their betters—or did we?

Here and there in little backwashes of the bushland were other moss-grown chimney stones—sad things, these tombstones of other people's hopes; the fragments of fine crockery, once the joy of a young bride, pretty buttons someone had worn, a little china hand, all that remained of a doll which had brought so much happiness one Christmas morning. Poor land, drought, bushfire or the rabbit wave had left its trail of ruin—now, across the years, relics speak of hopes and happiness and laughter that are no more. Only where the hardy fruit trees have survived, life, laughter and the shouting of happy children come back to the dead scene each summer with the ripening season. Perhaps fruit trees are the best of all memorials—the children and the birds will unconsciously bless you a hundred years after you have gone.

Blackfellow's Hill was a rounded, baldheaded, respectable-looking mountain on whom his giant neighbours looked down from their lofty and serene heights. He brought to mind a staid suburban businessman, quite an imposing figure in his own little circle—the small rounded hills of Long Swamp—and he looked down on them in much the same manner as big fellows looked down on him.

On the summit of Blackfellow's Hill was the grave of a blackfellow, who had been buried in the early days according to tribal rites; that the grave was hollow I have on the authority of a couple of young imps who, in the spirit of bravado, went up to dance on the grave one moonlit night—the booming hollow sounds which came from under their dancing feet sent them racing home like frightened rabbits.

On a little swampy flat which he had named The Scraw, betwixt the doorstep of Blackfellow's Hill and an outsweeping bend of the creek, Great-uncle Dominic McAuley had once lived.

Dominic was from Ireland and it must have been nostalgia which had prompted him to settle by that little lonely bog when far better land was available in his day. Maybe it was through loneliness that he peopled The Scraw and the surrounding ridges with various banshees, leprechauns, and other little people of his homeland.

That The Scraw had other uses than a stamping ground for leprechauns was demonstrated by Dominic's son, who, when he had merited a "lick of the stick," was wont to run out and stand on the quivering morass which would accommodate his light weight but would not support the old man's; here he had only to stay until parental wrath had subsided when all would be well again.

There were times when he was alone when the Little People used to set about disturbing Dominic's peace; his candle would suddenly go out when all was quiet and windless, or, at other times, horrible sounds would be borne on the night. Wretched nephews, silent as blackfellows, would sneak up to his slab humpy armed with long blowpipes of hollow pumpkin stems which they put through the cracks between the slabs, to blow out his candle, as the old man knelt at his devotions; or else they would disturb the night with weird groaning and other hideous sounds, with the aid of bullroarers and similar home-made gadgets. Dominic was never known to take umbrage at these manifestations; the doings of leprechauns and the like were above question and reproach.

There are no relics of Dominic's house. Back at the beginning of the present century there was a great cloudburst, which is still talked of around Long Swamp; the weight of water split a huge gash like a volcanic fissure from top to bottom of Blackfellow's Hill; down it rushed a terrifying wall of coarse sand, which fanned out many feet deep over the whole of the flat, burying Dominic's hearth-stone and The Scraw and the Little People for all time.

Exiled Trees

LOWER down the creek at the site of the former Cullen home were other fruit trees. What is it that is so breathtaking about fruit trees growing far from the nearest orchard? Maybe it's the small boy in us—always wanting to run off somewhere and live off the rich fruits growing wild in the bush. Whether or not we admit it, there is, somewhere in all of us, that urge to run away and live off the land; hence the eternal freshness and popularity of Defoe's "Robinson Crusoe." Sometimes, perhaps once a year, we sniff the spring breeze heavy with ozone, then, suddenly, we'd be willing to swap our big executive job, our bank account and our membership of the Yacht Club, all for a pair of dirty shorts, some fishing lines, a frying pan and a lonely islet in some forgotten corner of the Barrier Reef. Some—and I think they are the happiest people on earth—have done so. Many more of us would likely follow suit but for the ties of family, responsibility, convention and white man's burden generally.

The old Cullen place had other trees besides orchard survivals; there was a well-grown shrub of English box which had begun life as a slip from my own Dad's garden; tall and dense were the hawthorns, with their snowy clouds of honeyed blossom. Stranger exiles nearby were a small forest of American sycamore, but, if they were lonely in that land of Australian gums, they had at least one compatriot down the creek—a lofty pine which we had planted as a knee-high seedling on that proud day in 1908 when we opened our new mud-walled school.

We had moved down from our temporary school in Mr. Cullen's woolshed—the men and the older boys carrying desks and stools, medium pupils armed with maps, books and slates and the two tiniest ones, Philomena Cullen and I, carried the cane and the bell respectively. The choice of obedient Phil to carry the cane showed the wisdom of authority—apart from the fact that Phil was the lady and the cane was lighter, it would have run a dire risk of sabotage in my hands. As it was, the allocation of the bell to me proved unfortunate. I persistently rang it the whole two miles, to the annoyance of everyone but myself.

Exiled trees! I shall never see one without thinking of the exiled Australian gums of the Middle East and of one in particular which would have been the joy of Hans Heysen. It stood by a well in the semi-hostile village of Al Majal, at the hub of crooked, dirty, vile-smelling streets; it should have been on a ridge with the clean Australian wind stirring its limbs and white-faced cattle chewing in the shade. I looked around at my mates—tough, hard-bitten Desert Rats! There were tears in their eyes.

A superb row of Australian gums guards the war cemetery at Beersheba on the fringe of the Sinai Desert. We had gone there to pay homage and I'd found the grave of Major Billy Markwell, of our Queensland district, who fell at the battle of Beersheba in 1917. It is a far cry from the rich grasslands of the Logan River to the bitter wells of Beersheba. In a nearby row was the grave of International cricketer and demon bowler, Tibby Cotter, hero of my early boyhood—"When I grow up, I am going to bowl as fast as Tibby!" It was quiet there by his grave, but somewhere away in the distance I heard the roar of fifty thousand men at the Sydney Cricket Ground; then it faded and there was only the desert wind in the gums.

People speak of our war dead and their lonely graves in foreign lands, but those graves of Beersheba were not lonely; there was comradeship of death for those men who had fought and died together and only the spectator was alone and friendless. There can be no loneliness, even in a hostile land, where good Australian mates sleep together under the whispering gums of their homeland.

Down Long Swamp on Dad's old run is yet another lonely plum tree—a bearded patriarch which owes nothing of his existence to the tragedy of the passing settler—he got his start in a different way. Years and years ago, Dad was putting up a line of fence—and since they are so straight and true, he used plum rods as sight sticks. One rod thrust deep into the damp loam was forgotten, forgotten until the following spring when it burst into leaf and blossom. Dad's line of fence has vanished without a trace and has been forgotten a generation or more, but still the old-man tree lives on.

Quince Cricket

LOOKING once again, after a lapse of thirty-five years, at the site of Dad's old orchard in the bend of Long Swamp, where a couple of battered old warriors of fruit trees still hold up their heads, it came to me that this was once the centre of our world. More than anything else, fruit trees to me symbolise all future hope and the reward of patience; and how can future hope be better expressed than by a child looking up at the wintry buds of a naked fruit tree?

Some years ago a friend of mine, who went to call on a recently retired old gentleman and offer felicitations on his eightieth birthday, was surprised to find the object of his visit digging vigorously down on a little flat below the house. "I'm planting myself a little orchard," he explained. "I've been in the city all my life and never had a chance to grow my own fruit trees before. There'll be some apples and peaches and cherries and a lot of pears"—he paused and his eyes had a far-away look. "Pears," he said, "there's nothing I like better than a nice juicy pear." My friend went away feeling rather sad at the futility of what he thought to be an old man's last pathetic gesture against the inevitable; but he was wrong. His old friend lived to see the orchard flourish and, for fourteen summers, enjoyed the "nice, juicy pears" of his own growing.

That's what I mean about fruit trees—and why one way or another they always seem to be getting into my writings, often unnoticed. Our old orchard in winter was a place of enchantment, with its black lace against the sky and the windsong in its bare rods; a place of promise whose witchery was silently brewing against the day when the first warmth would come. Often we played under its dark fretwork and hopefully watched the sleeping buds until August brought first signs of their swelling; from then on we watched them daily until their pink and white splendour burst upon an awakening world.

I saw it all again and sniffed that lingering old-world smell and heard the shouts of youngsters and the throaty barkings of Lass and the drone of ten thousand bees; then the spell broke and there I was alone with just two old lichen-covered trees in the bend of a creek.

It was during the fruit-ripening season that the fair Eden in the creek bend truly captured our lives; it seemed that nothing could tear us far from those magic trees. When not gorging ourselves with fruit, we were playing nearby—under the willows, on the creek gravel or outside the fence where a white cart road wound through pale grass and yellow everlasting buttons.

It was here on this road that we played cricket to a code of local rules which would have shocked Wisden. These matches took place in Autumn when the best edible fruit had gone and we were reduced to hard quinces, indigestible to all animate creatures, save young O'Reillys. With a quince for a ball, an old kerosene tin for a wicket and almost anything for a bat, the game would be on; a new ball would be called for, when in the opinion of the umpires, the old ball was soft enough for human consumption. When there were enough old balls to provide every player with a soft quince, the innings would be declared closed and refreshments would be taken under the willows, after which the game would be on again. Perhaps the gravel, twigs, charcoal, etc., embedded in the quinces, in some way aided the digestion, because all who played that rugged game so long ago are still hearty. Quince cricket! I wonder is there some forgotten corner of the bush where kiddies still play it, or did the noble game rise, flourish and decline in that little bend of Long Swamp Creek.

Most of the popular kiddies' games of the period were played in the orchard, but there was yet another game with a peculiarly local flavour. This was a disgusting business, known as the

Cherry Scramble, which fortunately had seasonal limitations. The participants in this game took up stations in the limbs of Dad's big white-heart cherry tree and, at the word "go", crammed a dozen previously picked cherries into their mouths at one time. The competitor was not permitted to open his or her mouth until all of the pulp was swallowed—then the one who could spit out the largest number of stones was declared winner. In the case of a dead heat, the event would be re-run.

Somehow I can never think of cherries without thinking of the Man Who Wouldn't Die. You are not likely to find it anywhere in the annals of medicine, but, in our household, it was not considered wise from a gastronomical point of view to associate fresh fruit too closely with fresh milk. The minds of the younger people magnified this matter, until fresh milk on top of fresh fruit appeared to us as toxically potent as prussic acid.

This was the set-up when The Man rode in one day; he had some vague and long-forgotten business with Dad and, after its conclusion, refused lunch but settled for some cherries from a large basketful awaiting Mother's preserving pan. In businesslike manner he put away a couple of pounds of cherries and then asked if he might have some milk! Mother, who no doubt thought him old enough to know his own business, provided him with a jugful; the dreadful news was spread around and small children assembled, to stare saucer-eyed at the Doomed Man. There were two schools of thought on the matter, one which subscribed to the belief that the man would fall from his chair and die instantly, the other which held to the idea that there would be a minute or two of writhing agony before the end. However, the latent poison was not yet working when he rose to take his leave.

We followed him out to his horse and The Man, who may have been flattered at the size of his farewell committee, little dreamed that we had all assembled to see him drop dead. "Any moment now," we thought, as he cantered off up the cart road and we climbed fence posts the better to see him tumble from his horse; but that wretched man refused to die for us, and he cantered away out of sight just as though he had not drunk a quart of milk on top of two pounds of cherries. We were more shatteringly disillusioned that day than at the same time years later when the truth about Santa Claus became apparent.

Lazy Wind

UP the ridge above the old orchard beside where our pisé house of 1910 still stands are two old acacias. These are descendants of the ones which partly shaded our first slab house, which made cool pools of shade for the water barrel, for tied-up horses, for dogs, and for any member of the family who had an idle hour on a hot day.

The wooden bench in their shade was a favourite of Dad's when his "lazy wind" blew.

There was a breeze which came at times; it came from the east on the warm days of late summer. Nearly always it came in a good season. Drought winds came from the west; they were harsh and withering and brought choking dust from Australia's red heart, dust which grated on the oilcloth table cover under our plates at dinner time, which crept into our food and into every corner of the house, into our hair and into our nostrils, unpleasant dust which made the land-

27

scape remote and dirty and the sky a vast, low, pressing ceiling of nastiness, super-heated by a copper sun.

To Cullenbenbong the east wind was a benediction; the west wind a curse. The east wind brought a promise of rain, the lifeblood of all growing things; it brought damp coolness and the moist breath of forested coastal mountains. The west wind brought the threat of drought and desolation; there was a harshness in the way it rattled loose iron in the chimney trough; mournfully it rustled the withering leaves; there was a drab untidiness in the way it reversed the foliage of trees.

Dusty days had no compensations; the evenings were stripped of that pageant of colour which marches across the sky at sunset; dawn showed a dreary unpleasant landscape which looked as though it had slept in its clothes and risen without bathing or combing its hair.

Even the days of devastating bushfire were redeemed by their dawns and dusks of blood and imperial purple and their nights of red, angry splendour; but days of dust had none of the splendour which goes with bushfire; they were dreary and infinitely nasty.

Dad always called the gentle east wind his lazy wind; it came as a cool blessing when the day's heat was becoming trying and it made the bench under the big acacia a far more inviting prospect than any of those pottering little jobs which he usually loved to do. It seemed to infect neighbouring men with idleness too. Maybe the time of the year had much to do with it; it was that in-between time after Christmas, the shearing had been done, the early potatoes dug and all planting for the late crops was finished. Ahead in the soft haze of autumn days would be the bustle of the harvest, but just now was that late summer lull during which settlers used to catch up with odd jobs and hobbies or mend bits of fence or even sit in the shade by the water barrel as Dad was doing, smoking and reading the "Bulletin," to look up at times and contemplate his garden blossoming like the lovely wilderness which it was, or shift on the bench and gaze off across to the ripening corn of Triangle paddock in between the green V of willows which marked the joining of the two creeks.

There was one day long ago when, as Dad was doing just that, Old John came riding into the quiet of the afternoon, riding round the bend of Redfern Hill as unhurriedly as the lazy wind itself. Even at that distance you could tell it was Old John by the way he sat his horse—legs shoved forward like sulky shafts and the stockwhip coiled over one arm, by the full beard which matched the colour of his long-legged grey and by the black and white sheep dog of sorts which trotted behind, the whole adding a touch of quiet animation appropriate to the laziness of the scene. There was a squark and a clang as Redfern gate opened and shut, a splashing under the willows, a drink for the grey and a wallow for the sheep dog, and presently John reined up under the shade of the acacias.

"Gooday Peter! Come-ouder-that!" The final compound word was addressed to the dog which, bristles up, had gone to investigate Lass and Trix, lying heads on paws in the shade and too deeply imbued with the spirit of the lazy wind to show even a passing interest in their canine visitor. Throughout the district John's dog was known as "Come-ouder-that"—perhaps it had a name, but that was the only word John was ever known to address to it. The grey was known as Blue Spec, but the only thing he had in common with his famous namesake, the 1906 Melbourne Cup winner, was the possession of an identical number of legs, also a head and a tail.

John was looking for a red and white bullock—had looked everywhere, had Peter seen it? Peter hadn't.

Quite often neighbours had come along to ask about straying stock. There was the exasperated man who'd been looking for his horse—"looked for him for three days, and could find him no more than if he had opened up and swallowed the ground."

"Anyhow, get off and hang up your horse. Jane is going to wet the tea presently," invited Dad; but

John wouldn't get off and waste time drinking tea; John had to get on and find the bullock.

"Obegord no, I haven't time, Peter; Obegord yes, I must be goin'."

There didn't seem to be anything blasphemous about this "Obegord." It fell out easily and naturally as though this grey-bearded patriarch were on familiar speaking terms with his Maker.

John had recently been in Blackheath and was full of news, so he was still talking away like a box of galahs when Mother brought out a jug of tea an hour later. Yes, he would have some tea, but he hadn't time to get off his horse—"If a man gets off he'll stay all day. Obegord, no"; he "had to be goin'," so Peter handed him up a cup of tea and a buttered scone; and then a refilled cup and another buttered scone.

John was in too great a hurry to dismount, but he was still sitting across Blue Spec when the Imps came home from school and dispersed to get in the calves, to fetch morning wood, to bring cucumbers and tomatoes and lettuce up from the creek garden.

Slowly the great shadow of the Divide spread over the scene leaving Marsden's Rock a rosy island in a blue lake of twilight. Then and only then was Blue Spec turned out to roll in the barley grass of the home paddock, whilst Dad and John plodded up to the cart shed, John's bit and stirrup irons making sharp music against the deep, slow rumble of their voices.

It was a warm night and the men took their pipes and their yarning to the veranda after tea. The lazy wind had died to a whisper, a low seductive whisper which said "time doesn't matter." The air was heavy with roses and wallflowers; the stars were hazy and subdued and the voice of a mopoke was soft and far away.

It was with difficulty that the Imps were finally shepherded to bed—and at that they had to leave just as Dad was in the middle of swimming a mob of wild cattle across the flooded Abercrombie— how those cattle got on we never found out. Hours later, as the night sharpened and we sleepily pulled up the blankets, there was the thud of a log in the fireplace and far into the small hours the two old friends were mustering their scrubbers and yarding their brumbies and running the gauntlet of the myalls.

When the Imps left for school next morning Blue Spec was saddled and tied to the palings, but that deceived nobody unless it were John himself. Throughout the day the men consulted once more on the birth pains of young Australia, and drew blue-prints for its future—Australia would grow into a fine country if they had the running of it. Perhaps they were right. To what extent Dad would have succumbed to the wiles of the lazy wind without the advent of John is not known, but that hardly enters into the question. Dad had his duty as host. In spite of poverty and hard work, the period and the place had a graceful tempo of living and manners which seem almost unbelievable now. If a friend dropped in for a yarn, you wouldn't hear Dad say, "You must excuse me now, I must run along"; this held good whether the friend stayed two minutes or two days. Lass, Trix and Come-ouder-that had long since settled any differences there may have been and lay as immobile as the Landseer lions.

The lazy wind must have infected the Imps too; they were usually late home from school but that evening they were much later than usual; nor was there any surprise on their part at the sight of John sitting on Blue Spec and still insisting that he "must be goin', Obegord yes." True, he had allowed himself to be persuaded to dismount for the midday meal, but mid-afternoon found him back once more in the saddle ready to be "goin'."

The fires of evening flared redly and burned swiftly out, leaving a few smouldering embers away to the south-west; once more Blue Spec was turned into the horse paddock and the tinkling bells of saddlery sounded the way to the cart shed, and the men came slowly in to their tea.

They had finished with the floods and the fires. The wild cattle and wild horses and wild blacks were behind them. They had done with the early days of their country and had arranged its future;

but there was still the Messina earthquake—a very fresh memory—and a short step from there to the San Francisco quake, Martinique and the 1906 eruption of Vesuvius—then Pompeii and Herculaneum. The earth's central heating system was still getting a thorough going over when the Imps were chased off to bed, to be haunted by dreams of red-hot lava streaming down from Round Ridge and engulfing the homestead whilst they slept.

But something happened late that night, the lazy wind died; the night became sharp and still, the soft transparent haze cleared from overhead and stars and planets took on the hard, frosty glitter of diamonds. With a dawn of cold purple and the blue of glacier ice there were the whinny of a horse and the clinking and creaking of saddlery, and when the Imps came out to the washbench at sunrise there was a transformed scene. Gone were warmth and the soft grey haze of yesterday, the morning was clear-cut, sharp, and blue as a sapphire—the first heady outrider of autumn.

Blue Spec was saddled ready for the road and two men, damply combed of head and beard, impatiently awaited breakfast. But Blue Spec was not the only horse tied to the palings. Dad's black mare Zulu was saddled and a crowbar and shovel lent against the gate post; Dad was going over to fix that bit of fence at the back of Marsden's Rock and he just couldn't get his breakfast quickly enough. The opium-laden wind had been turned off and the two aimless, yarning cronies had reverted to their true selves—Australian pioneers, the toughest of their breed.

Everyone went out to see John off, and brave Mother, herself far too busy to hear the voice of any lazy wind, was true to the manners of her day and begged John to stay a little longer with us, even though she had been wishing him to Glory long since. But John really was going this time: "Must get home and get the corn pulled. Obegord yes." Mother was surprised, "But the bullock, John, what about the bullock?"

John's face went blank and for one awful moment it seemed as though he were going to say, "What bullock?" Then his beard split widely in a grin, "Oh, the bullock; he's sure to turn up all right."

The Hills of Megalong

IT was in 1911 that we left Long Swamp for good and settled temporarily in Megalong Valley until the day when we were to move on to our new home in Queensland.

Megalong was an enchanted land for young people—a lovely creek with many kinds of flowering bottlebrush, grevillea and wattle, low sandstone bluffs riddled with caves; one cave still bears my name, in charcoal, on its ceiling and a date in March, 1912. Above the bluffs were gardens of waratah, flannel flower, heath and boronia, with berries of wild currant and geebung for the inner boy. Higher up into the mountains were cool glens of treefern and sassafras, where the lyre birds and bronzewing pigeons lived out their lives, as in the days before Captain Cook.

Towering above this primitive Eden were the giant cliffs of the Blue Mountains, colourful, dramatic, different from the granite hills of my old home as the mountains of the moon.

These great walls, a thousand feet of red and yellow sandstone, slashed out by the remorseless machete of time, filled most of our skyline and our lives. The morning sun cut in gold searchlights through their battlements, the evening sun painted them with the glories of heaven.

With storm cloud, the mountains were black with frightening majesty; the booming from their cliffs shivered the cups on our dresser; then the storm would rumble off eastward and the sun break through to a miracle of wet gold cliffs and rising mists. For a brief and splendid hour, a hundred waterfalls would pour into the valley from the rock crowns which had a run-off as from a galvanized iron roof.

At one point where a small permanent creek found its way to the cliff edge, there was a waterfall which we called Smoking Fall. It fell a thousand feet from a beetling cornice of rock and, when the westerlies blew, as they did for nearly half the year, the uprush of wind against the cliff face lifted the waterfall in a cloud of fine smoky spray, hundreds of feet above the mountain, and blew it back to the source of the creek. Often it happened that the creek below the cliffs was reduced to a trickle, as the winds cut off its supply from above.

This new land of beauty and of wonders did not lay claim to me as much as it might have done in other circumstances. Like the Bedouin in Paradise, who often sighed for the blazing sands and bitter wells of his homeland, a large part of me was still amongst the singing oaks and sandy shallows of Long Swamp.

There was also another factor which over-shadowed the splendours and the novelties of Megalong. Letters had come back from Queensland where my brothers had found their own mountain paradise—a new land where the birds and the flowers and the trees were strange and lovely, a land which captured the imagination and stirred my feverish longings.

This was a land where we were soon to go and so Megalong became a dazed period of waiting and longing, less real than the past of Long Swamp or the future in that green wonderland of the North.

Megalong was my home at the end of an epoch, when the peace and the stability of the old order gave way to the thrill and the terror and the uncertainty of the new; not just in our lives but in all Western civilisation.

It was there on a sharp August day in 1914 that we heard the news which set in train a course of events affecting the destinies of all peoples of the world.

Peaceful Megalong was my home when the word "Anzac" was first written in blood and fire. But, somehow, when I recall those days, it is of the spinebills in the honeysuckle over the veranda that I think, or the wild duck which crashed our gleaming iron roof, mistaking it for a sheet of water in the dawn light. Or again of the night in 1913 when we celebrated the centenary of the first Blue Mountains crossing; our bonfire burning redly on the rock bench above the house and answering fingers of fire from a score of points along the black spine of the mountains.

Always, I will think fondly of the Hills of Megalong—the tea-trees and the white gums along the Nellie's Glen track, the glory of the cliffs above and the crash of their silent music—and, in the final count, the peace of God which comes where the big hills shut out the works of man.

The Haunted House—Part I

IT seems a long time ago now since that blue-gold day in 1917 when first I rode up through the valley that is Kerry. A mild sunny Queensland day it was as I rode towards those dark, mysterious mountains.

The Macpherson Ranges were little known then; the forbidding majesty of their cloud-capped mountains, their dark and awful ravines, their giant ramparts, and over all the lofty green gloom of their rainforests held a thousand mysteries in bird, orchid, and waterfall.

The Albert River, which through the ages had carved out the Valley of Kerry, had its birthplace in the heart of that dark, enchanted land, so it was up along this valley we must go to our own new home.

For years settlers had been pushing back to the mountains, their brush-hooks and axes had challenged the rainforest; the rainforest had fought back with the ripping thorn lash of its raspberry and lawyer vine, the torture of its Gympie stinging trees and the sear of its burning vines; but the main weapon of the forest was stealth and rapid growth. It grew whilst the settler slept, and when his money grew short and he went away to earn more, the green, greedy walls of the jungle would reach out to reclaim his clearing.

High in the heart of the range above the cliffs, my brothers had challenged the might of the forest and the rains and the loneliness. There I was going, a large boy in small pants—astride a chestnut horse, and with a packhorse in tow, going up to help take the place of three brothers somewhere at a war 14,000 miles away. Kerry was a lovely shallow valley with bluegum flats along the river and the ironbark and kangaroo grass ridges rising gently a thousand feet on either side.

There were many river crossings with swift rushing green water and smooth volcanic boulders. By the first river crossing was a house with grey shingles, a house almost screened by dark pine trees. There's a story about that house—a rather long one.

There in that house lived John Horan, a pioneer and a genial St. Christopher by the Ford, who kept an ever-open doorway for the flood-bound teamster or traveller, whether friend or stranger. No matter how long the flood lasted the traveller was commanded to stay, and whilst his horse or his bullocks were well paddocked, he himself would be eating well from fine china, for John, though a bachelor, was fastidious in his housekeeping and in his dress.

For many years John was accepted as Kerry's unofficial host. Travellers, writers—men in quest of "Colonial experince"—dropped in for an hour and stayed a week. There were the parties he gave when the wide verandas were screened with greenery and ferns; the cricketing dinners when the corks popped and fifty people sat down to roast chicken and sucking pig. There was the still-famous ball back in the last century when a special open-air dancefloor was laid out under the pines, a myriad Chinese lanterns lit the greenery, an orchestra brought specially from Brisbane made the music for two hundred guests who danced till the sun came over Cainbabel Range; there will never be a party like that again.

John, in his youth, had been the dandy of the district. Quite a few young men who later in life were well-to-do had borrowed John's splendid cutaway coat to be married in—the coat was returned after the ceremony, the honeymoon not being considered important as it usually consisted of travelling by horseback or dray to home—a newly-erected humpy.

There was a reason why John had remained a bachelor; there had been a lady long ago—at times the old man spoke of her and her beauty. They were to have been married and then the lady died and to John there was no one who could take her place. He lived on in the neat, white-latticed house alone, save when a night-bound or flood-bound traveller came his way.

Only once was his hospitality abused. A young loafer, finding himself on a good thing, decided to make it a welter; for three weeks after the floods had gone down to Moreton Bay he stayed on, usually on a veranda chair deep in a volume from John's well-stocked bookshelf, whilst his host, far too fine a gentleman to even hint that the lout had outstayed his welcome, attended to all of the housework in addition to the normal work on the property. But gentleman John, who had been watching his chance, found a way of speeding his guest; it was at the finish of supper at the end of the third week, and the loafer at last showing a latent spark of shame, decided to help with the dishes. He rose from the table, cleared and stacked the things:

"Where's your washing dish, Mr. Horan?"

"Washing dish!" John feigned astonishment. "I never wash up, young feller, the dogs do that for me.

"Here dogs, here dogs!" he called, setting down the plates on the floor.

Two big cattle dogs bounded in as though they had been a party to the plot, and enthusiastically wiped every morsel of steak, gravy and potatoes from the plates, the young man watching them the while, his jaw dropping like a barometer on the Coral Sea.

"Good dogs, good dogs," said John, as he patted their heads, picked up the Doulton plates from the floor and put them back in the rack.

"Ye see, young feller, there's no need for any washing up around here. The dogs do all of this for me."

The "young feller" slowly rolled his swag and walked off up the road towards the head of the river.

"Good dogs!" said John again half an hour later, as he gave them an extra feed before reaching for a dish and a kettle of hot water.

So through the years John kept his open house; timber teams rolled down the valley to the new railhead, twenty-four straining bullocks and high-wheeled creaking wagons heavy with the spoil of the forest, cedar, wine-red and perfumed like the nights of Araby, snow-white hoop pine straight and true as naval guns, and silky oak.

New settlers were pushing up to the rich jungle lands at the river head, more and more people were travelling the road and a goodly quota found their way under John's roof on nights of storm or flood. Teamsters, travellers and selectors came and went—so did the years, and at last in 1912 we find John an old man, an old man going blind. No longer could he keep his open house, he groped his way in eternal twilight; it was with difficulty that his simple meals were prepared and he saw the time soon ahead when the beloved house would have to be abandoned in favour of a home with relatives.

Then comes a strange part of the story. John, returning late one afternoon from his sister's house two miles down the road, "working his passage home" as he put it, found a queer-looking old man standing in the road outside his house. Something like a creation of the brothers Grimm this old man looked; he was small and thin with creamy-white hair almost to his shoulders, pale blue eyes, the skin of his shaven face pale and glassy, and the nose long and bent. The hands were bone covered with skin and the fingers incredibly long; but for all this air of antiquity the figure was not bent, rather the bearing was military. The old man's dress was nonetheless startling. Above nondescript boots and baggy trousers he wore an ancient swallow-tail coat of rusty green—people suspected that it had once been black—a faded stock at his thin and furrowed throat, and his cap, a coonskin cap of the Daniel Boone era, round and flat-topped with a foot-long tail hanging down the back.

He stood in the middle of the road, staring through the dark trees to John's house.

"Good evening, young feller," greeted John. There was nothing flippant about John's greeting even though the "young feller" seemed at least a hundred years old—that was his form of address to all men, old and young. The stranger made no direct reply; he gazed on at the house and then said in a slow, detached voice with an undefinable foreign accent—"Yes, this is the house; I've seen this house in a dream; it is the house where I am to die."

"Like Hell," thought John. "You'll do no dying around my place," and then his native hospitality came to the fore. "Come on in, young feller, and stay the night; 'tis getting late." He led the way through the trees and up into the house; he struck a match and gropingly felt for and lit a lamp.

"Your sight is bad," said the stranger. "I will stay and look after you."

Next morning before John was awake the stranger had swept and tidied the house, chopped wood and cooked breakfast. When John entered the stranger was seated at the table, but he immediately rose and stood to attention—this was his practice ever after when the master of the house entered a room. John protested unavailingly every time.

"What's your name, young feller, and where are you from?"

"My name is John Bahl," said the old man, but until that day years later when they took him to Kerry cemetery no one was able to find out where he was from or anything else about him.

So John Bahl stayed on—they made a queer contrast, those two old men who lived together— John Horan, blocky, bearded and running to fat;

John Bahl like one of Hal Gye's drawings from the Glugs of Gosh. John Horan radiating eternal good humour and good fellowship and smoking an eternal pipe; John Bahl, silent and reserved, outlandish and with an aura of mystery. That the stranger was eccentric was at once apparent; his ruling passion was the collecting of pretty scraps of blue-white rock crystal caught in the gravel wash of the Albert River; people riding down through the river crossing above the house would often surprise the old man bent over like a huge ibis as he fished for his little treasures. Thus disturbed, he would vanish like a ghost amongst the hanging bottle-brushes, not because of the inherent shyness of the man or his shame at being caught in such a childish pastime but because of his fear for the safety of his precious stones.

In fact he had been in the house a long while before he showed sufficient trust in John to show him the treasures; he laid them out with great pride and for the first time his calm was ruffled. "Look, John, my diamonds, my beautiful diamonds."

John picked up the "diamonds" and adjusted his failing sight to them. "Diamonds!" he snorted in disgust, "they're not diamonds, they're damned old stones."

The old man drew himself up. "I know a diamond," he said with simple and awful dignity. John bowed to superior knowledge.

So John Bahl went on, steadily amassing his jewels and storing them on shelves of a dugout up in a dry gully a hundred yards behind the house. That secret horde he revealed to no man, not even to John. In fact until the day he died he had shown it to but one man—John's nephew, Tom Ward.

It was a natural thing that the old man's hobby, appearance and dress should attract ridicule or good-humoured banter—young men and boys being what they are. Boys, not a little afraid of the gaunt old creature, would shout cheeky words from the safe backs of their ponies, and then gallop away. Very young men just old enough to be superior would ride up and offer facetious advice on the marketing of diamonds, or congratulate him on his fashionable attire, and then ride off laughing. Tom Ward befriended the old man and treated him as a human being rather than a strange and amusing zoological specimen, used to talk to him and cut his hair and do him other kindnesses. Then one day when Tom was up at his uncle's house, John Bahl beckoned him with a long and secretive finger. With all the reverence of the custodian of the Crown Jewels, he ushered Tom into the dugout and showed his precious treasures with the air of one conferring a great honour—as indeed he was.

The old man proved to be a socialist of kinds. John soon found that when he bought any article for himself he had to buy a similar one for his retainer and the latter always appropriated the best for his own use—new shoes or slippers, new eiderdown quilts for winter. "I will take the best one, John. I will take better care of it than you," and it was typical of John Horan that he allowed the old man to have his own way.

It was the coming of the war which brought some clue to John Bahl's origin. John Horan, who was a kindly, tolerant man, was speaking with disgust of the current intense and unreasoning hatred of all things German. Suddenly the strange old man who had seemed so unemotional, broke down and sobbed, then he spoke of the bitter oppression of German minorities in Alsace—how women and children were driven into streets on a winter's night. Presently he went to bed still weeping—he was a very old man and he was so deeply affected—could he have been one of those children?

There came a day in 1917, a black day for Kerry, when John Horan came slowly home at sunset with bad news—two Kerry lads had been killed in France, one of them his own nephew, Ronald Horan, the other Norbert O'Reilly (my brother); briefly he told the old man. "I'd rather," said John Bahl, "that you flogged me with a whip than tell me that." He went off alone in the dusk, weeping bitterly.

John Bahl had become part of the Kerry landscape; no one thought him odd any more, no one thought it clever to score off him; gradually he had been absorbed into his background and had become one of the Kerry folk. John Bahl down at the crossing looking for diamonds, or carrying his buckets of water or feeding his tribe of cats or sweeping busily with his broom was just an old man who lived in their midst. The war passed and the boys came home and the world settled down again.

Once more John Horan was coming home at sunset, "working his passage home," but this time there was no smoke from the chimney and no smell of cooking. He groped his way to the veranda. John Bahl was lying there, his two bony hands clutching the handle of the broom. John Bahl was dead. They buried him amongst the Kerry pioneers in that little hilltop cemetery overlooking Kerry flats and the winding Albert River. Next day Tom Ward took his horse and dray up to the treasure house and carefully loaded the "diamonds," half a drayful, which he took down to the cemetery and placed on the grave. There the old man lies, simply John Bahl—no age, no family, no country.

Things were not easy for John Horan after John Bahl had gone; he could cut his plug tobacco and fill his pipe, he could grope the way along the road with his stick and he could yarn by the hour; but the dim twilight of his world would not permit of cooking or simple housekeeping. John went down to live with his sister and nieces, but whether he missed his daily walk or missed his house, or whether it was just that his time had come—he was not long in following his old friend to the little cemetery.

The Haunted House—Part II

THE years were not kind to John Horan's house. As a rule, when a grand old pioneer is laid to rest under the gumtrees, the house which he cut from the wilderness will go on ringing with the voice of his grandchildren at their play, but John who had lost his love so long ago had only a silent neglected house to leave behind. A cyclone ripped the roof from the old kitchen; shingles tore loose and fell when there was no hand to nail them back; the rains and the decay ate the lattice and the veranda railings, the front steps sagged green and unsafe, dead leaves lay inches deep on the veranda, once so neatly swept, and night winds moaned through broken window panes. The pine trees, lofty and dense, made a dark shroud for the lonely, dead house.

Dead houses are things to stir our hearts and minds. They stand gaunt and spectral, their gaping windows like the empty eyesockets of dead men; the bats which stream out from their eaves at dusk, the gloom and silence of their nights, all tend to people them in our imagination with the ghosts of those who are gone. There are no quiet burial grounds for dead houses—they stand, decaying on their feet, the stark skeletons of their timber lifted to the suns, the winds and the rains of the years; sometimes a merciful vine will spread a green robe over the ruin, sometimes a merciful bushfire will return it to the dust of its mother earth, but mostly they stand, unhappy reminders of death where once there had been life, and silence where once there had been laughter.

John Horan's house was swiftly going the way of all dead houses, and perhaps because of the strange old man who had come there to die it soon acquired, amongst the young and imaginative, a reputation of being haunted. The young boys who had jeered at John Bahl and galloped away had grown to manhood, but of a new crop of small boys, any caught in the night by the first crossing would lie flat on the backs of their ponies and gallop madly by the house with never a backward glance.

The house *was* haunted, haunted by memories of hospitality and years of selfless service. On nights as I passed so often with my packhorse, deep thoughts of the past and the old man would stir me. Plodding along in the night with only the stars and the horses for company, I saw in my fancy the yellow light from the window and heard the sound of the talk and laughter. But because there was some of the small boy left in me—as indeed there still is—a well-grown young man didn't even look back either.

Time came when settlers who had once sheltered under John's roof drove by his house in shiny motor cars; time too when even I drove by in my first shiny motor car. It was a rich October day with the green of strong-growing corn along the Kerry flats, and the gold of the silky oak trees as they waved their arms in the wind which blows eternally downriver from the mountains.

Time came when there had to be a telephone to Green Mountains, built by the settlers. The wire was carried by packhorse and strung through jungles, over cliffs and down the ranges and, finally, out along the Kerry flats on its fourteen-mile journey to the nearest Government line. Part of my task was to carry a ladder on my back and put insulators on any big gumtree which grew somewhere near the line.

Came a night of strong wind and dark racing cloud when I rolled out my blankets at the crossing beside John Horan's house. All the weather wisdom taught by my father and learned in the years of my boyhood and manhood told me there would be drenching rain before morning. My common sense told me that close by there was a roof—an imperfect roof but a roof; still I lay there in the dark under the black clouds and the roaring wind and the writhing arms of the gums and bottlebrushes—a boyish fear of a dead house held me on the bank beside the river.

Came stronger wind with darker cloud and biting rain—enough of this foolishness! The blankets were rolled inside a water-proof ground-sheet and strong resolute footsteps brought me through a creaking gate and up between the dark pines to John Horan's house.

An uncertain moon was playing hide and seek in the rain-laden clouds, the wind was moaning through the trees and in the house, somewhere, a door banged. The moon went out and I stood in the dark of the pines; I turned away—it was harder to turn my back on that house than to face it. I turned to walk away, perhaps run away, but at that instant came cold driving rain and with it cold common sense. A fleeting moon again lighted my way up the weed-growth path; the first of the steps collapsed underfoot but there was easy access through a break in the veranda railing. I struck a match, the wind blew it out, another and another with the same result; that wasn't getting me anywhere, so after stamping around amongst the leaves to make sure that no snakes had taken refuge from the rain, I spread out my "nap" on the leafy veranda away from a drip and curled up for sleep. But sleep was not just yet—the wailing of the wind through broken shingles and panes, the queer relaxing of the house between gusts, the hiss of the rain and the steady "drrip—drrip—drrip—"

of the roof leaks—like the blood in a ghost story—kept me on edge. But a tired, healthy young animal is difficult to keep awake, so presently in spite of queer sounds, there was deep sleep broken finally by bird song in the pines and wet sunlight across the bluegum flats and the hills of Kerry.

Next day through sunshine and shower I went on putting up my insulators, mentally blessing John Horan for the comfort of his roof and his hospitality which had extended years beyond the grave; mentally thanking John Bahl, too, for not disturbing my dreams; my bedroll that night had occupied the place where he had lain in death clutching his broom, and none after had slept in that house.

The rest of my story is queer. I had come home that evening and boiled my billy beside the house, fried a pan full of sausages and cut the top from my last loaf of bread; a watery sun had dipped behind the Jinbroken Range; Kerry was uncertain with soft purple rain; then I saw the mailman coming. There was a letter—in a lady's handwriting—expected from Brisbane and all else was forgotten in my few bounds down to the road.

"Camped in the haunted house, eh? Aren't you afraid John Bahl will come and grab you in the middle of the night?" Bob Johnston, the mailman, said. I tried to think of something smart to say in reply, but remembering my panic on the previous night, words stuck in my throat.

It was dusk back at my campfire, a soft lilac dusk; the sausages were cooked—how well they smelt with onions—the billy boiled, the tea was made and tired legs were stretched out through the grass. Then for my loaf of bread—but it wasn't a loaf of bread any longer—the centre had been torn from it and there were marks as if bony fingers had hungrily torn away the inside of the loaf. I had been away five minutes—there were no cattle or pests, tramps were unknown; the country was open and even in the sunset light a man could have been seen for half a mile. I went on with my interrupted meal; fortunately my visitor, super-natural or otherwise, was not partial to sausages and onions, so there was still plenty to eat. That night and on countless hours since I have thought deeply of that evening and sought an explanation, but there is none.

Next day and on each of the four which I spent in the old house I ordered two loaves of bread a day instead of one, and at night I would put one by my pillow and one down at the end of the veranda. Then after a few prayers—too few—I would say in a loud voice, "Take the one down at the bottom, old boy—this one up here belongs to me." But during those days and nights, though I left all of my food wide open to temptation, not one crumb of my supplies was touched—to my everlasting disappointment. Maybe on that first night and day, through my selfishness in thinking of and providing only for myself, I had somehow offended the generous spirit which still warmed that blessed old house.

The Partnership of the Forest

TO me there is nothing in the Australian scene more dramatic than the sudden change from open country to the rainforest; and it still has the same element of shock as on that day back in 1917 when I rode up along Stockyard Creek flats among the gums and the kangaroo grass and first saw the high green wall of forest, beyond whose enchanted gateway all the familiar sights and sounds and scents of the Australian bush ceased to be. That arboreal frontier line has impressed itself upon all who have seen it and enquiring minds have searched for reasons why there is not a gradual merging of kinds instead of a sharply drawn line which neither may cross. All know that the rainforest follows the rain, but the mountain rains do not end like a ruled line drawn in a child's exercise book; the rains taper off gradually, the forest does not. There were people who attributed the sudden change of vegetation to a change in geological formation—investigation quickly proved this to be false. What then is the answer? This: that the forest is a vast co-operative affair, which maintains itself by the mutual support of many forms of life, few of which can exist individually. The units of the forest protect one another from storm and wind and excessive sun, they conserve moisture and preserve an atmosphere of eternal damp which resists bushfire.

There cannot then be any question of gradual merging of the forest and the grasslands—either you have rainforest or you have not. Neither can you think of the forest trees as a collection of individuals—they are all parts of a master plan.

It is possible to stand on a prominent hill and look out over a large expanse of Queensland rainforest without being conscious of seeing an individual tree. Perhaps you may identify an occasional hoop pine, towering darkly above his fellows, or a red cedar with his gold of autumn or red of spring, but in the main, treetops of the rainforest intermingle to form a continuous leafy blanket of dark green, which hides not only the earth below, but the trunks and branches of the trees themselves. The trees are brittle softwoods susceptible to damage from fierce winds which sweep the Queensland coastal mountains; they are so delicate that a breath of fire or even a single axe chop may spell their ultimate ruin.

The rainforest survives by the mutual support of its trees and their partnership with vines and other growths. The mosses and lichens, the huge clusters of orchid, birdsnest fern, elkhorn and staghorn form water reservoirs which help to perpetuate the humid conditions so necessary to the forest. The vines bind and stabilize the treetops by linking one to another; they thicken the leafy canopy above, shut out the sunlight and help to keep the forest cool and moist and so protect the delicate ferns, mosses and fungi, all of which in turn make their contributions to the general wellbeing of the forest.

The vines have other parts to play—they are the forest's first line of defence; and a tangled wall of wiry, thorny stinging and burning vine affords protection against intruders. Again, should an area of forest be devastated by wind a thorny and stinging screen of vine will quickly cover the ruin and protect the young trees springing up to take the place of the fallen giants. Many a settler in his small clearing has discovered to his sorrow that behind its advancing screen of thorny vine the rainforest is always moving in to reclaim his land. Some vines, then, are the shock troops of the forest. In this category come the lawyer and waitawhile, the wire vines, two species of stinging vine, five species of raspberry and the vicious burning vine, which inflicts painful friction burns on the unwary.

All other things being equal the forest will continue to advance across the grasslands; it works in a circle—more forest brings more condensation, which brings more rain, which brings more forest. Within reason this set-up might have greatly enlarged the forested areas but for the annual burning of the kangaroo-grass countries by the aborigines; this was done to facilitate the hunting of game which have a preference for the sweet, fresh feed engendered by the fire, but it also had the effect of checking the thorny screen which was moving out into the grassland. There is evidence that a great deal of our range country has been claimed by the forest within the last thousand years; this has all been made possible in the first place by a frontal attack on the thorny vines, backed up by the Gympie stinging trees and the prickly solanums.

Where conditions are favourable a single giant vine may spread across several treetops, may grow to a girth exceeding two feet and attain a possible age of hundreds of years. What are these monsters of the forest, so fantastic that it seems they should belong to another planet? Are they strange growths which belong only to the rains and the forest twilight—outlandish plants which have no counterpart in the rest of sunny Australia? No: for the most part they are rather ordinary vines which have reached their ultimate in development through favourable conditions and unlimited scope—the pepper, closely related to its commercial namesake; two species of raspberry, with edible berries, both of which are closely allied to the garden variety; two tecomas, either of which you may see blooming in suburban gardens; two wisterias, one with glorious blossoms, which will some day out-rival its imported cousin as a garden vine; a wild grape with bunches of purple fruit awaiting the magic touch of a new Burbank to promote it to the vineyard. It seems then that our giant vines are just domestic types running unchecked; for trellises they have the hundred-foot trees of the forest; their roots are deep in rich volcanic soil and the leafmould of the ages; they are watered by the big rains of sub-tropical mountains.

Let us first consider the pepper, the largest of them all and perhaps Australia's handsomest clinging vine. In dark sheltered gorges, far back in the Macpherson Ranges, I know of two peppers with a base circumference of six feet. What the ages of these vines are we can only conjecture, but we know that in the Old World there are grapevines which have been bearing for over four centuries.

Those of you who have seen the lovely wisteria at Admiralty House, Sydney, probably know that that vine is 150 years old, but it is only a puny youngster compared with the giants of the Queensland rainforests. At one stage of its growth, the pepper completely smothers its host tree in foliage denser and richer than imported ivy. It grows out along the main boughs and then hangs in thick leafy ropes perhaps forty feet towards the ground. The raspberries and wisterias, which may attain a girth exceeding three feet, are remarkable for the supply of water which they carry. A big vine, scientifically tapped, may yield a bucketful of pure drinking water, but the tapping of vines should be resorted to only in a case of extreme necessity, because the process is fatal to the vine and we should not lightly destroy a masterpiece which Nature has spent a hundred years in building.

The two tecomas, the magenta-throated bugle vine and the cream wonga vine spread over a large area of treetops and in spring similar areas of forest floor are carpeted in fallen blossom. The wild grape is one of the most tenacious of vines; it is a not uncommon sight to see fifty acres of forest with a continuous roof of tangled leafy grape.

The lawyer, perhaps the most notorious of Queensland vines, differs from the ordinary run of lianas. It is actually a vining palm, and a great tree smothered in its glassy hot-house palm-fronds is a sight so splendid that we may overlook its evil reputation.

No reference to beautiful vines would be complete without mention of the delicate vining fern of the mountain forests; a tall treefern, with its bole smothered in this lovely creeper, is a sight not readily forgotten.

When first you encounter the tangled vine masses of a great rainforest it appears as a chaotic jumble of disorderly plants, but when you examine this conglomeration and seek beneath the surface of things, you will find ORDER, the signature of the Architect of the Universe. You will find that certain forms are constantly repeated; the plants in their own way are obeying rules and conforming to a plan.

One of the first things you learn is that Nature works in curves; the straight line is the signature of man. You notice, too, that Nature abhors even numbers; you will find this expressed in a number of ways—in the veinings of leaves, the number of units in a compound leaf, the petals and other component parts of a blossom, the divisions of seed pods. There are, of course, exceptions, but some of those are accidentally caused. As far as our plants are concerned, Nature's favourite number appears to be five—often it re-occurs in blossoms and leaflets; next in popularity is the number three and, after that, the number seven. Another sacred law is the Law of Irregularity; search as you may in the greatest of forests, you will not find two leaves exactly alike. Yet another law is the one which provides that all vines climbing trees shall grow in anti-clockwise spirals; fewer than one vine in a thousand disobeys this ruling. (This, of course, applies only in the Southern Hemisphere).

The march of the forest across new land or in the reclaiming of a clearing is always accomplished in three stages. First, the thorny and stinging protective screen which I have already described. Second, the swift-growing, short-lived colonizing trees; various species of polyscias, melecope and evodia, acacia and duboisia. These in the main have a life span of around twenty-five years, but they afford cover and protection to the young trees which will form the third and permanent stage of the forest.

Not all of the colonizing trees are short-lived however; in their ranks is the hoop pine, the loftiest and noblest tree on our mountains; also the red ash (alphitonia), a handsome and useful timber, the soft bark of which may be used as a substitute for soap.

The duboisia has a place amongst our important plants—the drugs hyoscine and atropine are extracted from its leaves. Another duboisia in the West is the source of the aboriginal narcotic pituri. There is a tiny black beetle which eats the leaves of our duboisia—a drug addict you'd style him, and he is so highly charged with belladonna that should you accidentally get one in your eye, dilation of the pupil and temporary blindness will result.

The hoop pine already mentioned is also remarkable in that it is the only tree of our forests which is supported by a taproot; all of the other trees either have buttresses or depend on the mutual support of their fellow trees. To a newcomer the buttress trees represent an outlandish appearance. In some cases the buttresses may start from the tree trunk at a height of twenty feet and extend yards in the directions which give the tree a maximum amount of prop against the thrust of the prevailing winds. There are usually four primary buttresses and there may be a whole network of secondaries branching from them. Some of these secondaries, closely lapped, form water reservoirs which birds use in their drinking and bathing.

Other trees—notably the wiemannias—develop pockets in their trunks. These catch the run-off from the tree and drips from leaves and mosses, and even in dry seasons provide drinking water for birds and climbing animals. The forest provides food and water for the birds, the birds assist by the spreading of seed and the keeping down of borers and other insect pests.

The Fungi

OF all the growths of the rainforest none are more misunderstood than those underfoot children of the damp and the decay—the fungi.

The ruthless thorn vines and shrubs of the jungle and even the evil Gympie tree, Australia's worst stinging plant, command respect and grudging admiration, and we acknowledge their part in the reclaiming of fallen forest; but we don't like fungi.

Why? Maybe it is a long throwback to their association with witchcraft; to the mandrake which screamed when pulled out from its roots; to the asphodel, that pale lily of the dead. We are civilised and scientific now, aren't we? Could it be because there are poisonous killers in the ranks of the fungi? But we don't hate mankind because some men turn out to be murderers.

Again, could we dislike fungi because they are ghouls and coffin worms which live on the decay of their fellow plants? Yet all others, even the great trees of the forest, live on the decay of their fellow plants—fungus, the medium which transmutes the dead giant into the life-giving mulch without which the forest could not exist; it is the story of Omar's red rose which blossomed in the dust of a Caesar—out of death comes life, a story as old as the world.

Some say they do not like fungi because they do not conform to our usual standard of plants—that they have no leaves, no blossoms, no fruit, that they belong to the grotesque vegetation of a lost world rather than to our own sunny planet. But they have beauty and colour and graceful form; if, through prejudice, we cannot appreciate these things, the loss is ours.

In the darkest days of the wet season when heavy rainclouds brood over the mountains and the forest is a vast, gloomy dripping twilight shrouded in mist veils, when the colourful blossoms have gone and the colourful berries have yet to come—it is then that these lowly and despised people brighten your way with a variety of colour and form as entertaining as your flowers or your berries. Then at night when the great forest is as black as the heart of a coal mine, ten thousand points of green-white light come out to cheer you.

It seems that the fungi have power beyond that of the loveliest orchid, power to beautify the blackest night, to intrigue and capture the imagination as no fair flower of the day can do. By day a dripping wall of a jungle stream will be a show window of fern, palm, orchid and lily—beautiful in a classic and conventional way—but by night that same scene will be a fantasy; the carnival lights of the Little People will glow from their black velvet setting and reflect from the black mirror of the darkened water. With these, too, are other Little People of the darkness and the jungle, the myriad glow-worms, each lighting the jewelled web of his tiny cave amongst the mosses.

There is yet another joy of the night wanderer— the Milky Way fungus which comes with the big rains; by day it appears as a greyish white mould which binds together rotting leaves and twigs on the jungle floor; by night it glows with a misty, uncertain, nebulous light and the traveller gets an eerie impression that he is stalking in the darkness of outer space, with the Milky Way underfoot.

Our fungus forms vary from the huge woody brackets to the delicate tangled hair fungi, so fine that you must look carefully to see them.

It is up in the misty moss forests of Bethongabel and Wanungra that the bracket fungus achieves its ultimate in growth. There on the ancient Antarctic beech trees you will find brackets large enough to shelter you from rain. Each year they spread a fresh layer of brown growth on the underside, but this is so thin that one bracket which I have had under observation for twenty years has added so little to its thickness in that time that I have estimated its age to be over a hundred years—fungus a hundred years old. Compare that with the field mushroom which shrivels after a few hours in the sun. It would be possible only to make such a time test on an Antarctic beech; these senile trees survive mainly by drawing food from the decay of their own hearts. Any other tree of the forest with sufficient decay to give root to a bracket would fall and be reduced to mulch within ten years. Often in the big timber you find dead brackets lying on the ground whilst the tree which had once been their host has disappeared without a trace; but the beech, unchanging through the centuries, provides a host on which the bracket can live out its years.

On second thoughts—we rather like the fungi.

Mountain Magic

IN another book, "Green Mountains," I have told of the climb into the ranges, of life in the old humpy on Moran's Creek, of our first year of dairying and the carrying of cream by packhorse down the cliff track and the long miles out to Kerry.

The next winter there was the usual lull in dairying when the cows were dried off for the cold months and spelled until the coming of spring and the new calves. Mother and Rose, who had been with us, returned to Brisbane. Tom and Herb went off to work amongst the big pine trees in Cainbabel Gorge—helping to feed the ever-hungry sawmills and earning money to help in the future development of their selections. That left me alone with the cattle to look after, as well as a wonga pigeon, a batch of grey thrushes and yellow robins and a few scrub turkeys to feed.

It was a hard winter, dry and cold, and before August cattle were scratching for grass in the same clearing where the paspalum had been over their backs in the previous January; their foraging took them out to the kangaroo grass which grew dangerously close to the cliff edges between Moran's Falls and Balancing Rock. As long as the grass lasted I used to herd the cattle by day on the little neck of grassland which tapered out to Balancing Rock and so I became a "shepherd" boy of the mountains—my age a bare fifteen, my nearest neighbour far away below the cliffs three hours riding on a good horse.

Gradually the influence of the mountains gripped and took hold of me—alone like an eagle above the world; for company a vast and lonely land of mountains and ravines where even the cry of a curlew or the howl of a dingo seemed cheerful and companionable; doing nothing but watching the cattle, hearing only the distant thunder of waters from the green depths on either side, watching the lights and shadows change in the great gorge between Lost World and Moonlight Crag; then in the sunset driving the cattle back to the clearing, feeding my wild birds, building a big fire in the humpy, sharing an evening meal with Beelzebub the black cat, after which we would share the fire.

Though it was not then clear to me, I had tapped the secret of mountain hermits. It was not the same influence of mountains experienced earlier in my life at Long Swamp, it was something more demanding. Before that winter was gone I hated to see a visitor coming; sitting by my fire at night I would be greatly annoyed to hear a cheery hail from the ridge-top which told me that one of my brothers was coming home for a day or two—the ties of the mountain were becoming stronger than the ties of blood.

On rare excursions to the valley for provisions it became my practice carefully to avoid any horseman riding my way along the Kerry road; if he were ahead I'd slow down and let him get out of sight; if behind, then my horses would be pushed to their limit to keep him behind.

It was the return of my family with the coming of spring and the good grass and the baby calves which helped to break that grip of the mountains; but some of it persists even to this day. Once it has held you, even for a short time, its influence will always be felt—something which may fascinate you, something you may even hate but something which you can never ignore.

Strong indeed is the magic which the mountains brew. It rises in the cauldron smoke of the stormclouds which steam from their flanks with the rains; it is in the sacrificial fires of their dawns and in the dragon's blood which drenches them in their sunsets. They are bewitched by the jewelled blackness of their nights and haunted by the siren song and valkyrie shriek of their winds.

No sound of man or his works came to break the age-old voices of the ranges—the roar of waterfalls, the rush of winds, the scream of black cockatoos as they wheeled into the black of the rainclouds—voices which for ten times ten thousand years have sounded above the dark forests of my mountains. The splendour of the flame tree and the firewheel, the heady breath of orchid and jasmine—those were my ecstacies. The writhing might of the green tornado flailing its league-long arms across the ranges, the bellow of the storm gods in the crags and gorges—those were my drama and my grand symphony.

The influence of the mystic moods of the forest did not lessen with the maturing of my years. Many evenings in the walled blackness of Stockyard Creek gorge deepened the uneasy premonitions and the vague background of evil always there. The long dark miles along Cainbabel Range on nights too many to remember, where one twist of the track would bring elation, another acute depression, and then at times in the midst of a soliloquy a swift and nameless fear—to be gone almost in the same breath.

Then there were the footfalls, faint and almost unheard, which followed me on the forest tracks at night; when younger I investigated them, without fear and without result—now I just accept them as part of this fantastic world which is mine.

There is the unearthly glow of Min Min lights which sometimes hover above the timber at night and which have defied natural explanation.

These and other things bring the constant feeling that here in this area of wild, untamed, and untamable Australia we are closer to the essence of things—and that the barrier between us and the unknown is neither formidable nor far away.

Mountain winds weave their own spells, sometimes through association, sometimes through the scents which they bear and sometimes for no reason that we can put name to. The breezes of spring, rich with the blossoms of the forest and the call of a thousand birds, and that other spring wind, the warm north-wester with the smell of rain and a message of hope for all live things, these bring reactions which need no explaining. The strong, dry west winds of early summer which bring to me the feeling of gloom and desolation with a vague background of impending calamity—this could be a carry-back to boyhood; too often has calamity followed in their wake; they attended the great droughts of 1902, 1918 and 1919.

There are the cutting south-westers of winter which bring a tingling of the blood and a buoyancy of the spirits—a feeling that you want to jump over logs as you go down the paddock. These are the winds which scour the heavens and earth of all dust and haze and leave a vast and wonderful creation of bluebell skies and indigo mountains— perhaps the loveliest days of all, but if you would have this beauty you must accept the sharp and hurtful winds that go with it—a true symbol of life.

Haunting are the gentle east winds which come after the heat of fine summer days, driving spectres of low white cloud through the forests of evening. There is the wind blowing off distant bushfire with its mixed message of tragedy, and that most potent of all magic—the scent of burning gum leaves. There are the savage storm winds, which mingle fear and fascination in an intoxicating brew. These we understand, but there is another wind whose magic is not so obvious; this is the mother of the forest and the waterfalls, the cloudmaker, the lifegiver, the wind which brings the big rains, the south-easter.

This is the mystic wind of the mountains whose role as the giver of life has endowed it with the eternal enigma of woman. Subtle and mysterious are its spellbindings, inexplicable the nameless longings of the soul when the south-easter roars across the forest. Whether it comes with white walls of rain, or soft flying mist or just a cool freshness; whether it thunders or whispers, it brings a strange and lovely spiritual consciousness which troubles the heart and mind—a riddle of happiness and beauty and longing to which there seems to be no answer.

Deep in the rainforest beyond my house is a great rock to whose shelter I sometimes take my writing, when the south-easterly squalls are marching across the autumn hills. A dim leafy place it is with sparkling emeralds of rainwater in the green lace of moss and fern; often in a heavy shower it is shared with a yellow robin, a rufous fantail, a scrub wren or two.

Here in this retreat from the world, the troubled spirit of the south-easter seems to come closer. You hear the squall afar off as it rushes down from Mt. Bethongabel way, that dim land of cloud and moss and ancient trees; its voice swells louder as it comes, the forest waves its arms and tosses its head, crystal spears of rain stab the green—and then the roar moves on along the range, dying in the distance; gold searchlights of sun cut the dripping forest and the rising ground mists. Just a passing squall? There was more; there were voices on the wind as it came, chattering exchanges in a happy vein with sometimes a low shout—voices as of people in holiday mood where you caught an occasional lift of voice above the roar of the forest. Not any of the ordinary sounds—the bird cries, the scream of timber as tree rubs against tree—all of those sounds we have known so well and for so many years; these are voices. What are they; sounds, plucked, carried and distorted by the wind or twisted by the acoustics of my rock shelter and the big trees round it?

There is yet another spot, out among the big buttressed trees along Cainbabel Range, four miles away. This was once the end of our car road, where from 1934 to 1947 we met all cars and trucks with our saddle and packhorses. Those were the days of unbridged creeks and soft roads, and during the rains countless hours I spent there waiting for cars that came late or did not come at all. Cosy between the buttresses of a big tree—the firelight gleaming on br⬦it bars of rain and the wind roaring above, I'd wait. The voices would come with each rising gust, sometimes loud and fitful like the distant cries of children at play, sometimes desultory like those of people conversing above the clop of horses' hooves and yet so convincing that often I looked up the home track for a light and the people who must surely be coming. Again there were times when I heard the drone of aeroplane motors when all planes were grounded by storm and wind, and times when I heard the engine and grind of a car in low gear when the nearest car was stranded on the far side of flooded Canungra Creek, thirteen miles away.

Voices on the wind. Just another mystery of the mountains.

The Artful Dodgers

THE humpy on Moran's Creek which served as a home for fourteen years to 1926 was built across the boundary line of two selections so that it might fulfil the improvement and residential conditions on either block of land. The line went through the centre of the fireplace. Peter and Herb, the respective selectors, often had mock arguments in such terms as, "Come over to my end of the table and say it," "Put some wood on your part of the fire," or, "Get to hell out of my property."

The land laws of Queensland at the time provided that each selector, in addition to the effecting of certain improvements, should reside continuously on his land for the first five years. It is doubtful if any selector ever did; few selections—least of all in jungle land—became self-supporting within five years and few selectors had sufficient capital to hold out for that length of time. Almost without exception the men worked on their improvements whilst the money lasted, then went off elsewhere to work and save for a further effort.

Crown land rangers were sent round periodically to see that the law was enforced and any man not doing residence was in danger of losing his property by forfeit. Here a word may be said in favour of those rangers—it was due to their sympathy and broad interpretation of the law that many a man, to-day prosperous, was not driven from his land in his early selection days.

Back in those days when most bushmen were in the same boat—and were bound together as lawbreakers in a common cause—a "grapevine" telegraph used to go into action as soon as a ranger stepped off his train at the railhead. Very effective it was, too, in the times when telephones were luxuries enjoyed only by city people. Perhaps someone on the mail coach would drop a word at the right place; a man would saddle a horse and cut across a range to another house from which two more men would set out, riding in different directions—at other times and places it might have made a very effective bushranger set-up.

In a remarkably short time word would reach a road gang or a sawmill or a pinefeller's camp; tools would be dropped and horses grabbed; there'd be night riding on little known short-cuts across the ranges. Then when the ranger went his rounds every selection would be echoing with axe blows or choked with burning-off smoke. The ranger must have had many a smile to himself when he noted how fresh the origin of this hectic activity, or saw a sweat-caked horse sleeping under a tree, or perhaps tramped down weeds and grass which had grown high before the humpy door; but you may be sure that his report was in effect—"Men in residence, carrying on clearing operations."

There were certain little dodges that some men used to get up to if they wanted to get away from their district to some area where big money was to be earned; these little tricks didn't always fool the ranger but at least they had the effect of giving each party a satisfactory way out. In all South Queensland jungles you will find the marara tree—axemen have a more descriptive if less polite name for it—it is brutally hard to chop but, worse still, its core often contains wind cracks filled with inorganic matter resembling cement and guaranteed to take a big half-moon out of the face of any axe. For that reason mararas are usually left standing in the clearing after the felling and burning off; that and the fact that they make good firewood—strangely enough firewood is a big problem in that world of trees.

The mararas, however, had a third use; the trunk would burn green but burn very slowly—two months or more before it burned out to the branches. The artful dodger before leaving his district would fire a couple of green mararas and then ask a friend to ride up every couple of months and light some more. Apart from the peak of the rains, the dodger could be away for nine months and any ranger arriving within that time could conscientiously report "Burning-off operations on selection."

There was the delightful little one about the ranger who arrived at a clearing to find a padlocked humpy: that wasn't anything unusual—tramps got around and men often locked up before riding away for stores. The ranger peeped through the cracks between the slabs: there was a table where a meal had been eaten—an obviously dirty plate with crossed knife and fork, half a loaf of bread, an open jam tin and a sauce bottle. Hanging from the beam above was a wire gauze meat safe and on a plate inside the safe, a chunk of red corned beef.

The story should have ended there, but the official who had ridden from daylight was hungry enough to eat his horse; twice he cooeed loudly— no reply. He went around the humpy inspecting the wooden shutters; they were both fastened from inside but one was looser than the other; it rattled quite a good deal when shaken and finally after a lot of shaking the wooden catch slipped sideways and the shutter was free.

"This is breaking the law," thought the ranger, as he climbed through the window, "but a man can always leave a note; besides, hunger recognises only one law—the law of survival. Well, now for the 'scran'."

The "scran" did not look so appetising at close quarters; the plate wasn't very clean and the quarter-inch of dust on it didn't help either; the bread—what was wrong with it? Nothing much save that it was blue and as hard as blue granite; the jam was blue too, or rather what once had been jam was now shrivelled blue fungus. But the piece of red corned beef which had looked so tempting a minute before, could it be, yes, it was a chunk of red volcanic rock. The whole was an elaborate piece of stage scenery set up months before when the selector was leaving for the canefields a thousand miles north. The ranger forgot his hunger, collapsed on a stool and laughed until he cried. The story had a happy ending.

There is the story of another man who had settled away out in big gum country. A powerful young chap and a good worker, he put far more time and effort into his fencing and ringbarking than into his dwelling. For the latter he downed a stringybark tree, split it into slabs for the walls and used its bark for the roof; to save extra bother with furniture he had built the humpy around the tree stump so that the latter might serve as a table. "She'll do me till I can afford a real house."

The day came, as it came with most selectors, when money dried up at the bank and credit dried up at the store; there was a mob of cattle moving out from a nearby station, an extra drover was needed, so our lad strapped on his saddle-roll and joined them. When the mob was delivered three months later, he landed a good fencing contract, which lasted another five months. Heading home, well cashed-up and well pleased with himself, he just couldn't resist a sleeper-cutting contract, which he ran into on the way. "This'll put me on the pig's back. I'll be able to stock up and never look back."

At last he really *was* coming home, another fat cheque in his pocket and some uneasiness in his mind. A ranger had been reported in the district; around twelve months he'd been away against the planned three—still, there wasn't much to worry about, the place was well improved. At the township they said that the ranger had already headed out his way; that wasn't so good, letting him get there first; still, if a man put a spurt on . . . Just inside the home sliprails he saw that hurry wouldn't do any good, the ranger was already riding back.

"Hullo! You must be the ranger. Sorry I missed you. Just been to town to buy some terbacker. How about coming back and I'll boil the billy—of course, things are a bit rough at the humpy. No woman about the place yet."

The ranger grinned. "As a matter of fact they were a bit rough. No thanks, I'll be getting back to town."

They chatted for a moment about the weather, then the ranger went through the rails and away.

Long before he got near his humpy the selector saw that its roof had gone; a storm must have ripped it off shortly after he had left; but there was worse to come. With the heat and the rains, and its enclosure in a hot-box of four walls, the old stringy-bark stump had sprouted magnificently. Its suckers towered through and above the naked rafters until the whole show looked like a gigantic pot-plant. "A bit rough," but the selector had been on his land at inspection time and—well, he stocked up and never looked back.

Even back in Dad's time they had their troubles and though Peter O'Reilly was a God-fearing man he had often to resort to subtle strategy in holding his little bit of land. There was a grazing lease that he had and the rental had to be paid by a certain date, else all hell would stir. Working out alone without clock or calendar it suddenly occurred to him that his deadline must be approaching, if not already past. He wrote a cheque and a covering letter and dated both well before the deadline, but Peter, the strategist, was not yet finished. Deliberately he dogeared, rubbed and smudged the corners of the sealed envelope, then with a straw he extracted from his pipe stem some nicotine to add stain around the already mutilated missive. Hailing a neighbour passing on the way to

Lithgow, Peter entrusted to him the posting of the dubious looking letter.

The cheque arrived late and in due course Dad was hauled before the land court to show cause why he should not lose his land; he was on his oath, and in a bad spot.

"But I sent my cheque," protested Peter innocently.

"It arrived late," said the Bench. "When did you send it?"

"I cannot remember," witness answered truthfully.

"Did you post it yourself?" he was asked.

"No," answered Peter. "I gave it to a friend to post."

"Friend!" snapped the Bench. "He must have been a friend indeed; your letter arrived in a *filthy* condition a fortnight late and it positively *stank* of tobacco. Next time post your own letters."

"Yes, Sir," replied Peter, returning gleefully to his land.

It goes without saying that the young pioneers of Green Mountains also had their troubles in "doing residence." More than once when working away they had beaten the ranger home by a short head. But there was a time when local work was scarce and they were all back on the Blue Mountains, when a report came in to the Lands Office that the O'Reilly boys were not in residence. A ranger was sent to investigate. This time the grapevine was useless; good horses couldn't span the eight hundred miles and airliners were not even a dream of the future.

The ranger arrived and saw for himself—saw, too, the well-worn axes and brush-hooks and the clearings which had been won from the forbidding forest by that all-conquering combination, strength and hope, and the new slab humpies whose roofing iron had come by packhorse four-teen miles into the mountains. The ranger returned to Brisbane and at serious risk of losing his job, reported all well on the O'Reilly selections.

The Nights of the Kerry Dancing

THOSE were the nights! There'd be bubbling excitement in the afternoon, the polishing of shoes, the ironing of shirts and collars, a very serious ritual with no mother around the humpy; the flat irons were stood up in front of the open fire and then wiped carefully on brown paper before they were allowed to touch the sacred cloth; with collars it was trial and error— four would be starched and ironed and the best one taken.

Then there was the running down and the catching of sleek, shiny wild horses. You needed good horses. At its best it was a four-hour ride to Kerry Hall; along two miles of jungle to the plateau rim, down the old cliff track to the gorge, out through the long dark tunnel of jungle to Kerry road, then down along the bluegum flats and through many deep rocky crossings of the Albert River.

Maybe I'd have stores to bring back next day so it would be a string of packhorses that I'd be driving off in front of me as I rode off at sunset; fat shiny fellows, bucking with their empty pack saddles; I with my "good" clothes tied in a valise in front of the saddle, yelling murder at the horses as we raced through the jungle twilight.

Then the cliff track which struck awe even into the heart of a seventeen-year-old bushranger; blazing afterglow beyond the sawtoothed Divide fifty miles away, the heaving billows of purple country between, Ding Bing Falls back to the right, a silver ribbon tying the higher jungle to the lower, and just under my right stirrup over the cliff an abyss of dark green where a stone started from a horse's hoof brought back no sound or echo from below. Above, a gaunt cathedral of volcanic rock towered to the darkening sky, riddled with blowholes, the home of the great-eared bats, those black butterflies of hell which streamed out in their thousands to mingle their dark wings with the deepening gloom. Those were solemn moments even for a high-spirited youngster with high-spirited horses.

Deeper down the range we left the bats and met the owls, the nightjars and the frogmouths, who spoke softly through the coming night. Underfoot were snakes and maybe death adders, but who cared about them? Years later when riding through the jungle one hot night of thunder and lightning I lost my favourite horse, a lovely fiery roan, Javelin, through the bite of a tiger snake; he gave one mighty leap, then grew sluggish and then rolled over on his shoulder. Within twenty minutes that powerful little horse, which could and would run from dawn to dusk, was dead.

We would go down along the cutting through the gums where the blue possums chuckled and the koalas cried, where the night wind rustled the gum leaves and keened softly through the drooping she-oaks. The going would be slower there too; our horses, reared on the artificial grasses, paspalum and Rhodes grass, of the jungle clearings, would taste the sweetness of our own kangaroo grass, which grew breast-high to a man on the lower mountain. But there would be stars to cool your hot blood and stem your impatience.

With all of your famous astronomers thrown in, there is no man who loves his stars more than he who has ridden alone by night with his horses and his stars for company; the drover who rides his midnight watch around the cattle whilst the Milky Way wheels overhead; the Arab alone in his waste of drifting sand who steers his horse by the Dog Star and knows that he is going to a well, a well of bitter but life-giving water; the Australian pioneer or selector riding the night with his packhorse and his stars.

My love of stars came up from boyhood or down from my Dad. Dad and Uncle Frank were amongst the drovers who took the first big mob of cattle from Sydney-side out to the Channel country of West Queensland. Two years it took them. Some of the drovers fell from the fire-hardened spears of the myalls; some drowned in flooded rivers; some died from beri-beri. Often in blazing heat they sheltered their cattle by day and drove them by night. Perhaps it was because of Dad's tales by the fire that stars grew to be just as much part of my life as my meals. When later in life I had to take my part in war I looked to my stars rather than my illuminated oil compass to guide me at night.

So we would go down the range, the plodding packhorses ahead snorting, cropping and blowing pollen from their nostrils, and presently we would reach the bottom of the gorge and then there'd be the jungle, its deep dark tunnel of track, the incessant flicker of fire-flies and the glow-worms which shone from dark creek banks. Here the wild blood of the pioneers and the bushrangers would rise. I would yell and curse the horses, then we'd go down the jungle at a half gallop, the bucking packhorses in front with their saddles tearing through the vines, I lying flat on my saddle in the pitch blackness under the reaching arms of the jungle with its thorn vines and Gympie leaves. I don't know who enjoyed it most, the horses or I. It was still the romantic age for me; sometimes I'd be Ben Hur driving his chariot in the circus at Antioch, sometimes Ned Kelly and his band riding hard from the troopers; sometimes I'd be my father, Peter O'Reilly, riding for his life, with the spears of the myalls singing past his ears; but it was always a glorious ride.

Then we'd be out in the open again with the white stars and the white gums and the good smell of crushed kangaroo grass under the horses' feet. The smell of orchids which we had left behind in the jungle gave way to the smell of bottle-brushes by the river and that damp, watery, weedy smell of the deep dark waterhole down by the junction. The splashings through the river, the mile-long Kerry flats where we pounded along with the wind in our ears, and then the ridges where we got our breath and the breath of flowering bluegums.

Presently there would be the joining in of other young bushrangers, all well mounted and heading for Kerry Hall. More river crossings, more racing under the gums; the barking of dogs from each homestead, with perhaps a yell of "Wait for me!" and, whilst we waited, the rustlings and the scents of high tasselling corn.

Strange, it seems now, that although the dance was the one cause of all this mad night riding, the dancing was the one thing which left no impression nor anything worth recording. Though I remember Leslie Egan, who'd just returned from France, singing "Roses in Picardy," and again Ken Watterson singing "A Perfect Day," the dancing and music seem to have faded with the years, so that of all those nights of the Kerry dancing there remains only a symphony of rushing wind, of starlight and ghostly gums and the galloping hooves of horses.

Those were the wide open days when the big timber was still coming down the river; when sawmill hands, pine-fellers, bullock-drivers, new selectors and bush workers lent their colourful quota of "wild men" and "characters" to Kerry. There were the race days and the ringing-in of horses; when a man tried to outsmart his neighbour and outsmarted himself; when the owner of a hot favourite, which he wanted to lose the race, would rip the seams of the lead bag, only to be foiled by the clerk of the scales who had himself backed the favourite and called correct weight after the race, in spite of the missing lead. There were the free-for-all fights and there were the defaulting bookmakers, who were thrown into the lagoon.

Those were the days when if you walked up the steps into Kerry pub a big, hairy fist was likely to shoot out under your nose and a big rough voice say, "Smell the dead men on that," when a couple of bullock-drivers commandeered the pub sulky and played rickshaws up and down the road in the moonlight, one trotting in the shafts and the other sitting high in the seat urging on his mate with a truly magnificent flow of language. There was the time when the wild boys, hungry in the middle of the night and frustrated by a locked pantry, climbed the pepperina tree cum fowl roost and, with a bag of contraband poultry, had a glorious barbecue at a blazing iron-bark log a couple of hundred yards up the hill behind the pub. Then there was the never-to-be-forgotten midnight when, empty of purse and dry of throat, they crawled up under the floor of the locked bar with a tin washtub and an auger and, after a couple of experimental borings, hit the spare keg with a gusher which filled the tub.

Outside the dance hall and the pub, in those days before the coming of the motor car, there would be some sulkies standing shafts down, with their harnessed horses tied nearby, and there would be dozens of saddle horses tied around the fences. These soon received the attention of the wild colonial boys. First the sulkies would be wheeled up and their shafts put through the fence, then the horses would be brought around the opposite side of the fence, backed into the shafts and their tug straps fastened. When the owners came out to go home there were their rigs, all set to go—save for the little matter of a fence between the dashboard and the horse. Then the saddle horses would have their turn; a thoroughbred with splendid gear might have been tied alongside a poor old moke whose rat-eaten saddle had the stuffing hanging out. A switch of saddles was quickly made and likely the owner of the thor-oughbred, high with the excitement of the dance and a drink or two, wouldn't notice the difference until he arrived home the next day.

But those wicked men would not yet be satisfied. When a dignified pillar of the district came out to leave he would have near apoplexy at the sight of a lady's side-saddle atop his splendid horse, and a haughty lady who had somehow miraculously switched into a long riding habit would be horrified to find a boy's riding pad on her cob. Bridles and saddles were changed in all directions and often it was weeks before the gear was resorted; sometimes a fellow who had had the best of the deal was content to let things ride.

But Kerry isn't like that any more. The mills and the big timber have gone and the "characters" with all of their colour and devilment have gone with them. Nobody rings in horses any more or throws bookmakers into the lagoon; there is no one to turn loose a big carpet snake in the crowded bar-room or release a pugnacious frill lizard on the packed dance floor. No more are there fifty-odd horses tied around the fences to tempt the saddle-switcher.

Kerry is solid and prosperous and respectable now; there is a fine new hall and a five-piece orchestra; the roads are well surfaced and the rivers are bridged. Dancers arrive at the hall smoothly and silently in late-model sedan cars, and no one gallops by starlight on the nights of the Kerry dancing.

The Birds of Goblin Wood

L UCKY are the people who have fairies at the bottom of their gardens. We have a jungle at the bottom of ours, a jungle which stretches unbroken over seventy thousand acres of storm-breeding ranges and dark ravines. It is not merely at the bottom of the garden, it encloses us until it seems that the house and garden are at the bottom of a wide pit whose dark-green walls tower to the sun. There is but one window in the walls; it looks away across the blue of the Logan basin, forty miles to the splendid rock massif of Mt. Barney with its crags and towers—you have to go up to a thousand miles north before finding another mountain as high as Barney. Perhaps the seventy thousand acres of rainforest could be construed as part of our garden since it lies between us and all civilisation, from north-east, round by the east and south to the south-west. To the south and south-west where most of it lies, it is mainly trackless and much of it has yet to be explored.

A wild, untidy garden, the garden of Goblin Wood; the flowers, too, go reaching for the sun like the big trees that wall them in; foxgloves, dahlias and cosmos eight feet high; snapdragons with flower-spikes five feet high, which bow down with their own weight, touch the ground and rise again. A mad garden, everything growing wild and each crowding the other out.

"This is a madhouse," remarked a visitor, "even your front garden is at the back." True enough, the rear garden, which is netted, carries the best display of flowers; the front with its hardy and inedible plants is just as likely to be filled with wallabies or ponies as with flowers. On nights of wind and heavy rain wallabies shelter under the house and ringtail possums under the roof; birds too find sanctuary in the laundry and tool shed, under the tankstand and the eaves of the house.

There are fairies in our garden; here where the gloom of the forest yields to the sunlit works of man, the elfin children of the dark places come out and mingle with the little feathered people of the grass and the gum trees; the fairy wrens of the grasslands with their soft grey and glittering blue enamel and their friends the red-browed finches mingle amidst our flowers with the scrub wrens, those pugnacious little ones of the vines and mosses, and with the wee thornbills, the tiniest of feathered creatures in all our ranges. These little scrub wrens—the devil-birds—are capitalists on the backs of the workers; they follow feeding lyre-birds and log-runners and share in the insects and grubs scratched up by their hardworking hosts—even as the pilot fish shares the shark's meal and the jackal sponges on the lion. One thing that has always been a great mystery to me is how the thornbills keep themselves so well turned out in all weathers. After a ripping green thunderstorm, which twists the tops from the trees and leaves behind a foot of jagged hail on the ground; after a cyclone which blows at ninety miles an hour and spills thirty inches of rain in two days; when they have lifted and the first bar of green, gold sunshine comes down, there are the thornbills, not a feather wet or out of place, all turned out spick and span like guardsmen on parade.

Our garden is a democratic place; in the same tree you hear the warble of a magpie up from the gum trees by Moran's Falls, to be answered by the cry of a cat-bird from the green twilight of the Macpherson rainforests. Out under the giant blue-crowned hydrangeas by the tank a glittering paradise rifle-bird bathes in an earthenware pot under the tank drip; he steps out into the sun to shake and dry himself and in that shaking the many-coloured jewels of water fly from his irridescent body; they gleam for one glorious moment in the sun, then fall in wet splashes to the path, whilst the bird flashes briefly and splendidly to the dark of his home forest. That rare rainbow-coloured bird, the dragoon, will be calling "Walk to work!" amongst the dahlias, but he'll only be scratching there for land snails; he lives far back in the forest and the nest is built back in between the buttresses of a giant tree so that the rear and sides are stoutly guarded and only the front need be watched.

The regent bower-bird, that miracle of glossy black and dazzling gold—one of the most perfect works of the Creator—will perch beside us on the end of the kitchen table and peck his quota from a partly-prepared meal, whilst a grey thrush singing from the window ledge asks for a handout. Whip-birds build their nests in the big hydrangeas on the northern corner of the house and feed their young ones on our little bit of a veranda. There is never any need for an alarm clock—yellow robins with the first citron gleam of dawn above the black forest call their ringing "chop chop"; after that the whip-birds break out with their running crashes of music. Then comes the superb call of a golden whistler from the sassafras in the garden, followed by the "Quick, quick, quick" of log-runners scratching leaves under the treefern by the water tank, and then there can be no more sleep.

This partnership with birds began long ago, before Goblin Wood came into being. Perhaps it had begun at the old humpy at Moran's Creek in 1912 and maybe bird generations had carried on the tradition. But it grew and expanded from the day when first I laid axe and brush-hook to the forest in the cutting of that little rectangular clearing where my home was to grow. Thrushes, yellow robins and other little people of the forest, hungry with winter, applauded every axe stroke and dived in on every crashing tree to reap a harvest of grubs and insects. Then when the building plot was cleared and the pickings poor, the birds transferred their appetites to another front—down where the logs were coming in and the circular saw was whining in our little jungle sawmill, cutting the logs into boards for the building of Goblin Wood. Here worms were being ploughed up, while beetles, bugs and grubs stripped off in the bark by the saws became fair game, so everyone was happy.

When the holes for the pillar posts for our house were being dug, yellow robins wouldn't let the diggers alone and took worms and grubs from their shovels. But I was much too busy to notice my yellow robins in those days; digging, working, planning, and at night, when it was too dark to work, I'd be down the old Stockyard Creek track with my packhorses under the stars, packing back sheets of galvanised iron for our roof, cases of nails, lengths of gutter-piping and four-gallon tins of fuel to keep our engine running. There were things which wouldn't fit on to the back of a packhorse: six-foot glass windows, and curved galvanized iron to be made into the water tanks—

there was no chance of getting them around the cliff side on a horse's back so they came up the range on my back. There was a bathtub, too. I hope it has been used sufficiently to justify the initial effort.

Spring had come and the orchids were blooming when we came back from our honeymoon to our new house, a nice little house, smelling of freshly sawn silky oak, crow's ash and rosewood, but it was an empty house—empty even of partitions. Our mattresses, packed up from Stockyard Creek, were put down amongst the shavings and there we slept until I packed our beds up. Later came the three-ply boards for the partitions of our rooms and later still the pipes and taps which laid the water into our house. Many months went by before the last of our furniture came. It had been built in the factory—pulled down, packed up the mountain in pieces and then screwed together again. The most precious piece of all—Viola's full-length wardrobe mirror—I carried up the range on my back.

Little by little we got settled into Goblin Wood—sometimes a new partition, sometimes a new bit of furniture which had to be screwed together before it took shape—but steadily the flow came up the old cliff track.

Viola soon set to work establishing friendly relations with her jungle neighbours; young scrub turkeys from the last season's incubation mounds were coaxed into the kitchen and fed under the plank and trestle structure which was doing duty as a table until such time as ours arrived. Then one day they came in uninvited and broke two pieces of fine china, wedding presents which had been carefully carried up the mountain; as the china was decorated with a kookaburra motif perhaps some bird animosity had prompted the deed. "Blast the turkeys!" shouted the master of the house, chasing them with a broom; and they took to the big timber with a noisy flurry of wings. Five minutes later they were back on the "table" eating butter.

On through the months and years we fed our birds, and their fledglings which they brought along after each nesting. Came the day when our own little fledgling, Rhelma, was standing on the doorstep doling out bird-feed with a tiny pink hand—and by that time we needed an extra hand to feed them. There were mixed blessings in our bird-friendship. Viola's garden, her first very own, had its tall flower-spikes smashed down by bower birds in quest of floral decorations for their playgrounds. Lewin honeyeaters tore trumpet-blooms to pieces to reach the nectar, whilst the little lettuce patch suffered so heavily that we gave up trying to grow greens.

Too soon there came hard times of all work and no play—when our poor garden was neglected and wretched weeds and summer grass stretched across the paths and borders, when thistles grew blandly in the garden and wild tobacco seeded in the corner, but the garden became beautiful in a different way. Fairy wrens and red-browed finches swarmed in the seeding summer grass. The wild tobacco came alive with lordly king parrots in their scarlet, green, and butterfly blue, with friendly and comely brown pigeons, and the dainty little green-winged pigeons in their purple and green. But it was to the weeds and thistles which brought the crimson rosellas that we owed our greatest debt; the birds came by the score, dropping in one after another until the sky seemed to be raining balls of crimson fire. Our poor garden patch flashed with glorious colour—not static as in the ordinary garden, but colour that was alive with the poetry of motion. In the time of our greatest trial, when we had neither the heart nor the energy to tend our garden, the birds came and made it far more beautiful than it had ever been before.

Now I am planning a bigger garden with something of the same setting. There will, of course, be honeyed flowers for the spinebills and Lewins; but alongside there will be huge beds of Scotch thistle for the crimson rosellas, large areas of inkweed and wild tobacco for the king parrots and all of the rich-coloured fruit-eating pigeons. There will be beds of blue flowers blooming in rotation and paths paved with broken blue glass and china for the satin bower birds; gold flowers for the regent bower-birds and large areas overrun with summer grass where the finches, the fairy wrens and other little people of the grasslands may make themselves at home.

There will be shady places with deep mulch where the lyrebirds, log-runners and dragoons will come to scratch, and rotting logs with lots of grubs and centipedes where my grey thrushes will eat and sing, but mostly sing.

Each day a new plot will be dug so that the yellow bobs and Jack kookaburra will have digging ground. There will be lillypilly and pigeonberry trees for the catbird and the bower-birds; and a couple of dead borer-riddled trees to bring the paradise birds. There will have to be rats and mice in the garden too, for the mopokes at night.

Oh, yes, and some kikuyu grass and a few potatoes for the paddymelons and bandicoots and some grapes for the wee "flying mice."

Of course there will be flowers too—lots of sweet-scented, honeyed blooms to coax the splendid bird-wing butterflies.

Yes, it's going to be a queer garden, but a very beautiful one.

The feeding of our birds calls for no special technique. With the exception of parrots and pigeons, which are provided with grain, the universal handout is cheese. Even the magpies (whose fancy runs to raw meat) and the yellow robins and thrushes (with a favourite diet of grubs and worms) have taken to their new food with a relish; it seems that almost anything from a mouse to an elephant likes cheese.

It is natural that with such numbers and varieties of birds on the dole some friction should arise in the feeding; the slogan "Might is right" still holds good, so we have an order of precedence based on size and pugnacity. At the top of this list we have the black and white magpies which clear the deck when they come to feed; the only birds which do not flee the field are their cousins the currawongs, which, however, are easy-going and never seem to make trouble for their smaller neighbours. Next on the avian ladder is the grey butcher-bird, a meat eater by choice and a cheese addict by accident. His black-and-white cousin, whose superb flute calls may be heard around the clearing, either scorns our dole or doesn't know of its existence. The satin bower-birds in numbers and greed usually dominate the scene; only one lesser bird, the regent bower-bird, stands his ground when their hordes invade the feeding place—his greatest fear is the female, who chases him from the ground and will not allow him a crumb whilst she feeds. Next in order are the grey thrushes which "stand over" the yellow robins, which in turn bully the Lewin honeyeaters. Yellow robins arrive four or five at a time—"Sideways perched upon a stake, eloquent appeal I make, spare a crumb for pity's sake" as C. J. Dennis put it. On equal terms a Lewin will hold his own with a yellow bob, but the latter usually gang up on him. Below the Lewins we have the courageous and wicked-looking little scrub wrens—devil-birds— the yellow-throated, he of the artistic moss nest draped all through the rainforest, and his smaller cousin the white-browed. Back in the forest they scold at every human being who comes their way, but here at Goblin Wood their scoldings usually indicate the presence of a cuckoo or a snake. Recently a chorus of angry chattering led me to an eight-foot carpet snake draped in a honeysuckle vine by the fence. A dozen devil birds, not content with merely vocal demonstrations, were flying, beating their wings and snapping at the snake's head; the snake could have swallowed fifty of them without taking the edge off his appetite.

Lesser than the devil birds are the dainty red-browed finches which come by the score to the feeding ground, dropping from the trees like falling red and green leaves of autumn; with them the fairy wrens feed amicably. It is a constant joy to watch the fairy wrens feeding—the proud little blue man, the grey boys and jennies all bouncing along the bricks like tiny feathered balls. Perhaps Bluey is all the prouder because of the period of humiliation which he endures in the changing from his grey to his splendid adult suit of blue enamel and black; during the change-over period he is a pathetic, moth-eaten creature whom no one loves. We have noticed here that when Bluey first gets his adult plumage he keeps it for six months, loses it for three, then regains it for good.

Of the birds which acquire adult plumage the slowest to change over seems to be the regent bower-bird. In the case of one which changed last spring it was three months before the gold head feathers reached perfection. On one occasion a newly promoted purple satin retained one drab feather in either wing all through summer, but this must have been a freak.

At the bottom of our dole list are the tiny thornbills. These wee brown elves swarm in the shrubbery and feed on minute insect life, but every now and then, when the deck is clear, they descend to the bricks and pick up crumbs too small for any other bird to manage. People apart are the parrots, which come in flocks and eat their grain whilst interfering with no one; turkeys, which come in the early morning, have their one big meal, and mind their own business for the rest of the day; the unobtrusive brown mountain thrush, which comes out from underneath the floor, glides through ferns and flowers, does her feeding and spends the day around the place without getting in the way of any other bird; and finally the little green-winged pigeon appears, walking primly and nodding her head like a nice little old lady as she goes all unruffled through a ruck of snarling, gobbling bower birds.

Then, of course, there was Guy; Guy was a tawny frogmouth, a pet and an importation. Not that we haven't frogmouths here; there are plenty of them around and years ago we had another as a pet, a fallen fledgling. There was a pet magpie in the house at the time and the two became friends of a kind; but they were an ill-assorted pair; the magpie keeping the frogmouth awake by day and the frogmouth reversing the proceedings at night; their feeding times were similarly staggered so that it was a great relief to us when they were both old enough to live off the land. Guy came from down Ipswich way; he had evidently been blown from the nest by a violent storm on Guy Fawkes Night and next morning, hurt, wet and hungry, he was found by Mary Powell, daughter of the chaplain at Amberley R.A.A.F. Station. Mary fed and cared for her charge and gradually over three months some sort of order began to emerge from the untidy ball of fluffy feathers which had been Guy. Here Mary and Guy reached the parting of the ways; the Reverend Mr. Powell and his family were returning to England and a place had to be found for the bird, some place out bush which would offer a maximum chance of advancement to an up and coming frogmouth.

So it was that Guy came to us; he was getting big, there was unlimited natural food to tickle his palate, soon he would be able to live off the land, but Guy, who knew a good thing when he saw it, had other ideas. At nine months of age he was still hand-fed on raw meat and spoon-fed all his drinking water; perhaps civilization has softened the bird or perhaps through association he has learnt guile from his betters, the humans.

From a couple of incidents which occurred, it would almost seem that Guy had retained some of the influence of his Rectory days. One night when a few of the lads were playing poker in the dining-room the bird flew in through an open window, landing in the middle of their table with a terrific pounding of wings; he knocked the card deck and the chips to the floor and he broke up the game just as effectively as if he had been a police squad. The cove with the three aces was not amused! Another time when a few people were taking a pre-dinner "spot" Guy flew in and knocked over a glass of sherry—would have upset the bottle, too, but for the presence of mind of an interested party. Guy was normally the most placid of creatures, but should you make soft owl noises deep down in your throat, he would suddenly stiffen and streamline himself, and become, not a bird, but the broken branch of a dead tree; he would keep this rigid pose indefinitely and it is easy to understand how frogmouths out in their home bushland can melt into their backgrounds until it becomes impossible for human eyes to distinguish them.

Quite apart from our feeding of birds, there are those of them which supplement their rations by following our various occupations and cashing in on them. Killing days bring magpies, currawongs, kookaburras, butcher-birds and sometimes a grey goshawk, all in search of the bits and pieces not wanted for human consumption. Most of these birds will at times attempt to gate-crash the fowl-feeding; or if the hens are being fed on grain the parrots will try their luck. If you are gardening your first upturned spadeful of earth will ring the yellow bobs in strength; if sweeping or raking leaves and rubbish there is sure to be a large following of devil-birds, which normally live on the small surface insect-life. The woodheap is an eternal source of attraction for our grey thrushes; at the first sound of axe blows they arrive chirping and singing in the shrubbery nearby, then dive amongst the flying chips for grubs, worms or borers which are always present in the dead jungle timber; and then, after they have had their fill, they stay around and entertain with their glorious calls. In these foraging expeditions the thrushes are usually led by Baby, perhaps the sauciest and friendliest of all our "dole" birds. Baby always keeps a critical eye on the woodheap and seems to know what it is all about when we take out the blitz wagon for a new load of wood; on our return she will meet us a hundred yards from home and ride back on the load feeding as she goes. We have many thrushes around the place and they all look pretty much alike, but a few of them have personalities strong enough to impress themselves upon us. Baby was a product of the second post-war thrush generation—her parents, Dad and Mum Thrush, are still with us—now, to complicate matters, Baby's baby, Baby II, has a grown-up brood of her own, so we are losing track of family relationships. The grey thrushes are the only feathered people here who will come for their tucker when called; we give a certain whistle which they will nearly always answer before they come. At times when hungry they will come to a nearby tree and loudly tell us all about it, then when we speak to them in a certain tone of voice they will keep answering and singing until fed.

Our best-lived thrush was Crookedbeak. He came to us as a hungry fledgling just turned loose upon the world; the world is tough enough on fledglings at any time, but Crookedbeak had an added disability—the lower mandible of his beak was split and each half turned outward, making it almost impossible for him to collect his food. Viola coaxed him on to the kitchen window ledge and fed him. He took his food with great difficulty at first but, finally, by turning his head sideways he was able to get enough to eat. He would never take his place in the crowded queue on the window ledge, or compete with the hungry horde on the brick path; rather he would wait until all other birds were fed and then shyly approach; after feeding he would linger on the window ledge or on the sacred bamboo outside and make deep little gurgling sounds which took the place of the thanksgiving song which his disability would not permit. So through that autumn, winter and spring he stayed with us and prospered, but it was noticeable that with the coming of warm autumn and the resultant influx of insects he foraged and became more dependent upon himself. Then in the last days of November there came a crashing green hailstorm and when the ice had melted from the forest and the wreck of our garden, Crookedbeak was gone. Sadly we wrote him off as one of the casualties of the storm. Summer and the Big Rains came and went and so on until after a chill night in late April we woke to find our lost bird once more on the window ledge. It is difficult to describe our happiness in the wanderer's return—it was partly I suppose the fact that we had saved his life and helped him to take his place in the world which gave us such an interest in him, but mainly it was because his fondness for our company was not just a prelude to food—after feeding he would stay around in the sacred bamboo for as long as we cared to talk to him. Maybe his disability had in some way cut him off from his fellows and he was lonely. His disappearance following the hailstorm might have been a coincidence or perhaps the poor fellow had been kicked around so much by fate that a barrage of ice was just too much. The latter theory is partly borne out by the fact that two seasons later he again disappeared for his summer jaunt after a heavy hailstorm. To our great joy, on his second return he could sing for us. Somehow he had mastered the early shortcomings—but he continued to make the queer little gurgling sound as well. So year by year Crookedbeak wintered with us, leaving us late spring and returning in late autumn, and Goblin Wood celebrated an annual day of rejoicing—the Return of Crookedbeak. But last season, his sixth, we watched for his return from the first sharp days of autumn to the hard frosts of winter, but our bird came no more. Poor Crookedbeak! I hope he has found a land where it is always spring and the grubs are fat and plentiful.

Brigands in Satin

LIKE the poor, the satin bower-birds are always with us. At times they make themselves unpopular by their destruction of garden greens and flowers, and by their bullying of lesser birds which come to feed at our doorstep, but nothing can disturb that place which they occupy in our minds; the thrill of finding a new playground and its treasures is as fresh and new as it was in the day long ago when we discovered our first one. The minor heartbreaks of finding delphiniums, larkspurs and lupins smashed and ruined by the birds' ruthless quest for blue flowers, or a lettuce patch stripped by their ever-greedy bills, have their compensations in many different ways, not the least of which are the imperial beauty of the adult male in his purple satin coat and the consciousness that we are playing host to one of the bird wonders of the world.

The satin bower-bird is not only a thief, but apparently a thief without honour amongst its kind—it steals another's trophies without compunction; a bird flying over another bird's bower will take a fancy to a piece of blue glass and carry it off to his own bower, only to lose it next day to a third. A tiny blue eye-lotion bottle which I had under observation changed bowers four times within a week.

The birds and their playgrounds are plentiful in our area; many of the stolen and re-stolen treasures go the rounds of the local bowers. Some go far afield, step by step and are never seen again; still others return, like some echo of the past, after a lapse of years. One summer, down in a bower near Moran's Falls, I found a fragment of china with a deep blue stripe; it was a fragment of a bread-and-butter plate which Mother had brought up to the old humpy in 1917; the plate was broken and I had forgotten it for over thirty years. A few days later it was gone again—whither this time? Will future bird generations be playing with that fragment of Mother's plate and winging it through the rainforest long after the last O'Reilly has gone?

Another little wanderer from the past was Rhelma's first baby comb which turned up in a playground seventy-five yards from the house. A blue comb it was and so tiny that it had become obsolete before Rhelma was six months of age; it had been missing for seventeen years. It stayed a few days and then vanished once more. Then there was a big, blue, glassy marble of Rhelma's, which she had named Pinkle's Eye—in deference to the family cat. Pinkle's Eye disappeared from amongst a score of marbles on the veranda one day, and turned up in a nearby bower some twelve years later.

But my favourite bower-bird story concerns little Kerry Clancy, the forestry ranger's daughter. In a tiny clearing two miles on through the rainforest at the forestry camp where the Clancy's lived, there was a wail one morning when baby Kerry discovered the loss of her toy motor car, a little blue plastic creation which had been a present for her second birthday. Daddy went the rounds of the bowers and brought back the car with a warning that if the birds got it again they would be allowed to keep it. The warning was forgotten, the car was left outside and again it disappeared—this time completely; it was in none of the bowers around the clearing. Some time later the Clancy's left the district and the toy car was not seen in the area in over two years. Came the day when the Clancy's returned to Green Mountains for a visit and went out to look once more at their old camp; and there, in a bower some twenty yards from where it had first disappeared, was Kerry's little car. It was in perfect condition. The birds had carried it around and played with it for more than two years and had taken good care of it. Kerry was quite happy to leave it with them. "They've been playing with my car and they love it."

No trouble seems too great for a bird in the securing of fresh blue flowers for his bower each morning; deep back in the forest I have found bowers decorated with fresh blue coleus from the cliffs, more than a mile away. At sunrise one morning we found where a blue lupin flower—the first of the season—had been snapped off and taken away, but on the ground beside the stump lay a fresh purple-blue coleus which the bird had brought from the cliffs a mile away. In flying over our garden he had seen something that he liked better, and leaving us his hard-got wildflower by way of exchange, he took our lupin. One of the queerest twists of the bird's collector's habit is his penchant for onion skins, and no well-stocked bower near civilization is complete without them. The laundry is a favourite hunting-ground and there is a perpetually open season for blue bags and dainty blue handkerchiefs. Some time ago a nice little city visitor did some washing and pinned it out to dry with blue plastic clothes pegs; later she found her dainties lying on the grass; her pegs are still going the rounds of the local bowers. At times guests who leave their windows open are mystified by the disappearance of blue combs and tooth-brushes, and I am always dreading the possibility that someone may leave a blue sapphire ring unguarded. Our most ambitious bower-bird was the one which took a blue felt hat belonging to my sister Rose; anyhow, crime didn't pay, for the hat became entangled in a mass of wild raspberry just above the playground so there were no fun and games with that hat.

It is a deeply satisfying thought that some things which had once been cherished by us are not buried in rubbish tips when they are broken or have outlived their usefulness. I am thinking here of Mother's little plate, of Rhelma's comb and marble and of Kerry's toy car, which are still being cherished; thinking too of many another well-loved piece of china around the bushland which will be treasured by some bird, long after the original owner has been forgotten.

Small Flakes of Stone

ONE day at the cliff edge by Moran's Falls I saw beneath my feet a dull sparkle from a small chip of stone. The comings and goings of many sightseers had worn threadbare the carpet of kangaroo grass, big rains had eroded the red earth and had brought once more to the light of day a tiny relic of those forgotten men whose land our forefathers usurped. It had lain there buried perhaps a hundred years, perhaps a thousand—men and forests come and go but a flake of quartzite belongs to the ages.

There were many others to follow and every year the wash from the rain exposes more. The top of Moran's Falls would seem to have been a favourite camping place for the dark hunters of long ago; how else to explain such large quantities of their crude stone knives and scrapers, all brought from distant mountains, for none of the local rock was suitable for implement-making. The spot, in spite of its inaccessibility, had much to commend it as a camp site to a small hunting party, a sunny, grassy ledge which must have attracted wild life from the great forest towering beyond; there were good firewood, an everlasting stream well stocked with eels, and a glorious view down the ravine across the rolling ridges to the far blue peaks of the Divide. It seems to me that the view would have played a part in the lives of the aborigines; primitive peoples are generally more mountain-conscious than we are. They venerate mountains and endow them with powers for good or evil; fantastic as some of their beliefs may have been, it would be useless to try to explain away the powerful influence of mountains.

The stones, about an inch across and designed for a thumb and forefinger grip, are in some cases as sharp as the finest steel knife, but whereas steel will disappear in rust after a few short years the little flint knives will hold a cutting edge for ten thousand years after their owners have blown away in dust. Above the camp site, on a ridge that leads up to Moonlight Crag, is a huge dead tallow-wood tree bearing a scar where a large sheet of bark had been stripped off to roof a gunyah. Some years after the bark had been taken—at least a hundred years ago—the tree was killed by lightning and so the scar, which had begun to heal at the edges, is preserved to this day, together with the toe-holds, chopped out with a stone axe, which enabled the climber to cut out his long sheet of roofing bark.

The tribes whose territories abutted the Macphersons seldom climbed beyond the foothills and then, as far as is known, they kept to the open grass country. There seems to have been both practical and superstitious reasons why the high tops with their damp, dark forests were taboo. To a sun-loving people the cloudlands of Mt. Wanungra and his lofty neighbours would have been an uninviting prospect, and to a people whose camp fires played an all-important part in their lives and ritual, the damp smouldering firewood of the big forests would have been anathema. Yet right through the ranges, on their highest crests and in their densest forests, wherever dislodged earth or uprooted trees enable you to see beneath the leaf mould of the centuries, you may find the signature of the stone-age man, the small sharp flakes of cutting stone. Under the ancient beeches of Mt. Bethongabel, where a two-foot cutting had been made for a forestry track, I found sharp cutters of grey quartzite which probably came from the Birnam Range, thirty miles away. Another and deeper excavation yielded me a superb chip of agate veined with grey and blue, which apparently came from much farther afield. Did these ancient wanderings antedate the superstitious awe of high, dark places or did they belong to the far-off days before a change of world climate sent the great, green forests stalking across the Macphersons?

In my tiny "museum" at Goblin Wood are two sharp cutting flints side by side. They are very similar and on appearances might both have been the work of the same man. One came from Snake Ridge, about two miles away, the other is a Palaeolithic flint which I found by that cradle of civilisation, the Mediterranean. One may be two hundred years old, the other may be twenty thousand or more years ago. One was fashioned by a wild black man, the other by a wild white man.

Strange that the coming of the road which was to bring modern car and bus traffic to our mountains uncovered a lost page of the past history of the aborigine. A bulldozer cutting eighteen inches into the soil on Snake Ridge, a couple of miles away, uncovered a large number of flints and four little stone axes, rather crude and unlike the types in use at the coming of the white settlers. From the amount of stuff which I recovered in the brief time before road metal sealed down the excavation, it would seem to have been a well-patronized campsite; and the depths to which the relics had been silted over seemed to indicate considerable age. It would be interesting to speculate on the possible age of this lost camp, but very rash to pass any judgment.

A queer echo of age-old taboo came to our mountains when Charles Chauvel came on location with his film company to "shoot" the mountain sequences of the film "Sons of Matthew." The script called for an aboriginal stockman for the droving scenes and Chauvel secured the services of Roger Bell of Hillview. Roger was a full-blooded aborigine born on the Logan River, one of the last living men of the district to have been initiated according to tribal law. At seventy he was healthy and industrious and a good horseman; he was cheerful and had one of the heartiest laughs I have ever heard. Roger joined us on location up under the mountains at the head of the Albert River and seemed to enjoy his new work of film-making. Roger was good company by the camp fire and his extraordinary laugh was so infectious that it never failed to touch off the whole company, but deep under his merry and rather commonplace exterior the coals of tribal mysticism were still alive. One day during one of those interminable waits which we had learned to associate with the making of motion pictures, the talk turned to roarers, those flat pieces of notched wood which in expert hands produced such strange noises and terrifying sounds at the sacred bora ceremonies. Dad used to make them for us long ago and on moonlight nights their fearsome moaning would sound along the flats and the ridges of Long Swamp. In a nostalgic whim inspired by those faraway nights, my sister Rose turned and spoke to Roger who had been listening without speaking.

"Roger, I would like to have a roarer, will you make me one?"

"By'm by," said Roger, but the tone of his voice and the strange dark look which came into his eyes told very plainly that the mysteries of the Bora Circle were not for the amusement of white people.

Location was changed to Numinbah Valley at the head of Nerang River; this was a more or less similar layout, a narrow river valley flanked by mighty, wooded mountains. Again Roger seemed happy in his work during the weeks which we spent there. At last when the company packed up and prepared to move up to the top of Green Mountains for the culminating sequences, Roger suddenly became difficult and said in effect that he'd had enough of moving pictures and wanted to go back to Hillview. All he knew of the new location was that it was up at O'Reilly's and, well, he didn't want to go up to O'Reilly's. After much argument and coaxing he finally decided to go, provided that it wouldn't be for long. At first his objections seemed to have been based on a state of being "fed up" and generally out of sorts, but when he arrived on the range top after a journey through long dark miles of forest, the life seemed suddenly to go out of him. There was terror in his eyes and he would not eat or speak, just went to his bunk and stayed there. In the meantime, unknown to us, the few remaining old people of Roger's tribe who had heard of his journey up on to the mountain were saying, "That's the end of Roger; he's gone up into forbidden country." When it became apparent that Roger was ill, he was taken home by car, but he pined and quickly died. No white man knows what killed him; no one ever will.

But Jessie Brown had known. Jessie, who spent her last days in Beaudesert, was a very old aborigine who had mingled the knowledge of the twentieth century with the secrets of the Stone Age.

Jessie told of the time long ago when her mother had died. The onset of her mother's illness had been so swift that there had been no time to send for her people, yet they had arrived in time to see her alive; this meant that most of them had started their journeys well before the mother had become ill. Pressed to tell more about this, Jessie said they had been warned by their totem, the green tree-frog; but, of course, this could have been an evasion.

Jessie went to see Roger when he was dying. What he told her no one will ever know for Jessie now is dead, but this she said:

"Our people know. Roger go to some place he shouldn't go; he see sumpin; he die."

"What did he see, Jessie?"

Jessie's deep dark eyes became long corridors of fear. "Sumpin," she said; "he see sumpin."

Down in the lower gorge of Stockyard Creek, where the rainforest gives way to the bluegums, the ironbarks and the kangaroo grass, there is a level flat up above the creek which was probably the last "natural" camping ground of the local tribesmen. Two or three of the older white settlers who were trusted were told of a sacred stone which was brought to that camp and buried there. It was the custom to keep the stone buried and to dig it up on rare ceremonial occasions. The strangest part about the sacred stone was its weight—though smaller than a man's head it was said that the strongest of men could not lift it unaided. It seemed that with the twilight of their tribe at hand a final resting place had to be found for the stone and there is little doubt that it is buried deep on the flat up above the bed of Stockyard Creek.

With the passing of the stone and the men who guarded it there was much speculation among the settlers who had known of its existence. No white man had ever been allowed to see the stone, so that in guesses as to its nature one person's idea was as good as another's. It was thought that the stone might be of some metal—even gold—which would account for its weight, and there had been half-hearted suggestions about digging it up, but the flat is a couple of acres in extent. A more up-to-date school of thought could launch an expedition with a geiger counter in case the lost stone was a chunk of uranium.

However, there is no metalliferous rock in the Macphersons or in the whole of the Logan and Albert river basins. The nearest mineral field is in the New England Range, over fifty miles away, and one cannot visualise the transportation of such a heavy object through strange tribal lands where trespass meant war and death. My theory, and all theories must have the same value, is that the stone was a meteorite, which would account for its existence far from a mineral field. That, too, would account more readily for the mystic significance attached to it, for even had they not known it as a fiery visitor from outer space, its great weight and the bell-like ring which nickel iron gives off when struck would establish it as a thing of wonder among those childlike people. There is plenty of precedent for the veneration of such stones—the sacred Kabba stone in the holy of holies at Mecca is a meteorite.

If my theory is correct, then the lost stone could be located with the aid of a standard army mine detector, but I find myself wondering if that should be. Should the sacred stone be unearthed and thereby add a little more to our pitifully small knowledge of a lost people, or should it be left for ever where the old men buried it for safekeeping in the last days of their tribe?

Norbert's Last Message

THE lines below were sent by my brother Norbert to the Kerry girl he had hoped to marry. They were written in France and arrived in Australia weeks after the news of Norb's death had come by cable.

CAINBABEL CREEK

Thoughts come to me as I wander
  With a loose and drooping rein,
Thoughts of days gone by and ended
  Flash into my mind again.

When I rode in blissful silence
  With a heart too full to speak
There was one who rode beside me,
  By your banks, Cainbabel Creek.

Crooning streamlet full of beauty,
  Banks of darkest emerald green,
Tiny waterfalls that ripple
  Over rocks with silken sheen.

Fig-tree branches softly clustering,
  Blending green of every shade
With a harmony more perfect
  Than e'er human heart has made.

And there rushes swiftly o'er me,
  Memory that is almost pain,
As there comes the fresh, damp perfume
  Of those fig-tree boughs again.

Cainbabel, you're watching dearest
  Haunts me daily like a spell,
Calls me back again in spirit
  To the spot I love so well.

Brings me back when I am weary
  The peace of soul I vainly seek,
Though I never more shall see you
  Peaceful, cool Cainbabel Creek.

                    Norb. O'Reilly,
                    August, 1917.

Cainbabel Creek! Where the great Moreton Bay
figs with their lofty gardens of staghorns reach out
from either side and span the cold clear water. It
was there that the young pioneers rested and
drank deep, then shouldered their hundred-pound
packs and marched on to their green mountains,
buoyed up by that unconquerable combination,
youth, strength and hope.

To Norb, Cainbabel Creek meant peace, green
coolness and rest—a place to lay down a burden. It

is easy to think how it filled his mind as he went up
to die in a hell of shellfire on that red August day.

Alex. Chisholm's Discovery

IT was the November of 1918, when our family lived in the old humpy on Moran's Creek and we were just getting used to the idea that the Great War had really ended. A letter came from Brisbane in the mail—it was from the secretary of the Queensland Field Naturalists' Club, proposing a Christmas camping trip to the new Lamington National Park, which had been gazetted three years earlier. It was proposed that the main camp should be in the Antarctic beech forest at Mt. Bethongabel, 3,800 feet above sea level.

In any normal year the choice of camp site would have been unfortunate—Mt. Bethongabel spends much of the summer and autumn under a hood of cloud, and its annual rainfall average is in the three-figure category—but in 1918-19 period fell the severest drought in the history of our district, and so for once Bethongabel was a pleasant camp prospect. A fortnight before Christmas there was much packhorse activity. Tents, camp gear and stores had been sent up to

Beaudesert by train, ahead of the party. From Beaudesert the gear had been brought out fourteen miles by the Kerry coach. Tom and Herb packed up most of the gear. Mick, who by this time had been discharged from the A.I.F., also helped in the work, though he was still convalescent.

The Kerry coach ran three times a week, taking cream to the Beaudesert butter factory and returning in the afternoon with empty cream cans, groceries, meat, bread and mail. A stop was made at each man's cream stand—a low-walled sentry-box affair. At each stop the driver half-hitched the reins to the brake pedal, so that the brake would be pulled on should the horses take fright whilst the driver was not in control. Normally four horses pulled the coach, but the road was an unmade strip of bottomless black soil and in wet times five and even seven horses were needed. At the time of the first Field Naturalists' camp Randall Silcock was the coach driver; later my brother Herb owned the run.

A few days before Christmas the naturalists arrived in Beaudesert by mixed train and were taken by coach to the Kerry hotel, where they were lodged for the night. Next morning Herb turned up with the saddle horses, and the party rode on up the river flats. They turned into Stockyard Creek gorge, climbed the old cliff track to the plateau and so on out through the seven miles to Mt. Bethongabel. It was a full day's ride.

Included in the party were veteran etymologist, Henry Tryon, ranked amongst the world's best men in his field, and Cyril White, Queensland Government botanist, who was a grandson of the great botanist Manson Bailey. As a young man White had accompanied Bailey on a New Guinea collecting expedition. There was Brisbane businessman, W. H. Herman, well known as a collector in Barrier Reef conchology. There were also two gentlemen of the fourth estate—in their capacities as naturalists rather than pressmen. They were George Harrison of the "Brisbane Courier" and Alex Chisholm of the "Daily Mail"—two newspapers which have since merged. Both newspapers later carried articles telling the splendour of our ranges. "The Queenslander," a weekly journal, also carried an illustrated article by George Harrison. In the "Sydney Mail" there later appeared a profusely illustrated article by Alex Chisholm. The article was headed "The Green Mountains of Queensland." There we saw, for the first time in print, the name by which our range is now known. It was Henry Tryon who had proposed the name. Said Tryon, "New South Wales has its Blue Mountains, there are the Green Mountains"; and never was a more appropriate name coined.

We knew Alex Chisholm as the final authority on all things ornithological in Australia. We knew him, too, as an author, and as the man who compiled and edited that monumental work, "The Australian Encyclopaedia."

With dawn, on the first morning of the camp, and the ancient forest ringing with bird calls, Alex Chisholm was out along the bridle track, mentally classifying the bird music as it came to ear—living in that private heaven of an ornithologist in rich new country. Then suddenly from under the treeferns, in a tangle of vine and wind-fallen debris, there came a sound which was not music. It was a resounding "chuit—chuit chuit chuit chuit, etc.," about eleven times. It was as fast and as loud as submachine-gun fire, but on a higher key; at close quarters it disturbed and irritated the eardrums. Through the leafy cover the watcher caught the vague outline of a smallish brown bird.

Alex Chisholm dredged his mind for ornithological facts and finally came up with that kind of diagnosis which is ever a source of wonder to the layman. There had been but two species of bird to make that kind of sound. One had lived in the big Karri country, south-south-east of Perth, and was considered to be extinct; the other had lived near Tintenbar on the Richmond River of N.S.W., but had vanished when its habitat, the great rain-forest, had been put to the axe. This second species was also known on Dorrigo Plateau, but it had not been heard there in twenty years. The West Australian species was atrichornis clamosus, or noisy scrub bird. The N.S.W. species was atrichornis rufescens, or rufous scrub bird. Alex Chisholm deduced—correctly—that the bird he was listening to belonged to the second species.

A report of Alex Chisholm's discovery soon came under the notice of H. L. White, a well-known Hunter River pastoralist and ornithologist, who had spent a good deal of his considerable fortune in the collecting of native birds and eggs for scientific purposes. His huge collection was destined for presentation to an Australian national museum which he hoped would one day be built at Canberra.

In charge of H. L. White's museum and library at Belltrees, Scone, was naturalist Syd W. Jackson, who had been responsible for the collection of many of the specimens. Jackson had undertaken many collecting expeditions financed by White. Amongst others was a journey to the tableland rainforests of North Queensland, in quest of the toothbilled bower-bird; to a Tasmanian mountain lake, for the bluebilled duck, and a long and fruitless search of the big Karri country of West Australia in the forlorn hope of finding a survivor of that lost species, the noisy scrub bird.

Both White and Jackson had vivid memories of the rufous scrub bird. Though this bird had been discovered and described by Ramsay in the previous century, no female had been collected. Jackson had been on two expeditions in quest of the bird—one to the Richmond River and one to

Dorrigo Plateau. On the latter he secured a clutch of eggs, but still the female eluded the collector. Now, at last, it seemed that the time had come for White to complete his collection and close the book on the rufous scrub bird.*

*After a lapse of sixty years the noisy scrub bird was re-located early in 1962, to the north-west of Albany, Western Australia.

S. W. Jackson—1919 Camp

LETTERS came from Belltrees and others were sent in reply, and so in the early spring of 1919 Jackson arrived on the plateau, three of our packhorses laden with his gear. A tent was pitched for the naturalist in Mick's clearing, beside the humpy, and Herb was installed as cook, guide and offsider. We had been looking forward to Jackson's coming—expecting some long, lean bloke with leggings and perhaps a pith helmet. It was something of a shock, then, to meet a big, heavy, middle-aged man in an expensive suit and a cloth cap, and sporting big Edwardian moustaches waxed at the tips. There were more surprises to come. In spite of his bulk, Jackson could glide noiselessly through dense rainforest when stalking birds, and he could walk the average bushman off his legs in the course of a day.

Once in camp, Jackson shed his glad rags in favour of old camp clothes, and delighted in having himself photographed with a week's growth of beard. He took his turn at cooking and baked excellent dampers in the camp oven.

Jackson's permit for the collection of certain bird and egg specimens was the only one of its kind ever issued in respect of a national park in Queensland. It is extremely unlikely that one will ever be issued again, but it was considered desirable at the time, since scientific description was then incomplete. The naturalist had come well recommended; not only were there letters from H. L. White, explaining the importance of the mission, but there was also a letter of introduction from Premier Holman of N.S.W. to Premier Ryan of Queensland: a letter which stated in part that "any courtesy shown to Mr. Jackson would be taken as a compliment to the State of New South Wales."

In that spring of 1919 Jackson collected a female of the species atrichornis rufescens, also a male which was seen to differ a little from the parent species. It was at first classed as a sub-species of the original, but sub-species are no longer recognised in ornithological nomenclature.

By early November the squeeze of the 1919 drought was approaching its climax; the Albert River had stopped running through Kerry and became a series of weedy waterholes, alive with cod, catfish and eel. Cattle in the Logan and Albert districts were dying by the thousand. Herb found it necessary to see to the well-being of our dry stock, and so for three weeks I took his place in Jackson's camp. I was just past my sixteenth birthday, and my world was a very wonderful place—dark singing forests that called with a thousand voices; great cliffs that fell away to the far blue country; spirited horses, and many, many miles of exciting bridle track.

Jackson had finished collecting—he had given up hope of finding an atrichornis nest that season, and was devoting his attention to photography. In his typical painstaking manner, the naturalist had picked the subjects and the forest scenes for his photographs weeks before. He had taken his big camera—empty—to each prospective picture site and lined up the scene through his focusing plate—there was even a little peg to mark where each leg of the camera tripod was to stand. All of this had been done whilst awaiting suitable photographic weather. Jackson favoured an evenly clouded sky and a long time exposure for rainforest subjects—this also presupposed a dead calm, since a moving leaf, fern or palm frond would mar the picture. Each photograph was in its own way a work of art, and the greatest insult possible to Jackson would have been to refer to his pictures as "snaps."

Much of my time was taken up in the carrying of a big leather plate-bag, and the lunch, and posing in the pictures when it was necessary to have a human figure for the purpose of scale ("Note man in righthand bottom corner"); the position of the man had been predetermined, and a little peg marked the spot where he was to stand.

Our water for all purposes was carried from a spring deep in a gully, two hundred yards from the camp. The spring flow was daily weakening from the drought; it took half an hour to fill a kerosene tin, four gallons, and the photographer needed about twelve gallons a night, over and above domestic use—those sacred plates were washed and rewashed after developing and fixing.

By the time the last of the plates was put away to dry, our Big Ben alarm clock would have shown 11 p.m. and I would roll into my bunk, but sleep was not for my companion; his journal had to be written up and after that his correspondence—he corresponded with biologists right across the world. There were times when his light burned until 2 a.m. Once a week I saddled up and rode fourteen miles through the early morning, to post Jackson's big wallet of mail; I usually returned with a large swag of incoming letters.

At dawn, on nearly every morning, I walked down to the home clearing for milk. The track paralleled Moran's Creek for half a mile through rainforest in splendid treefern country. Perhaps the drought had brought in a far larger bird population than was usual, along the water of Moran's Creek, or perhaps it was that the world was so wonderful then, and I was so much in tune with it, but it seems to me now, in looking back from this distance, that the morning bird calls along that forest track were richer and far more numerous during those three weeks, than I have at any other time experienced. The crashes of the whip-birds overlapped each other, the drawn-out whistles, which preceded the crashes, and which varied over an octave, formed a continuous flute orchestra in the background: on every side the forest rang and re-rang with the chop, chopping of yellow robins, with the crystal-sharp calling of the golden whistlers and with the mellow notes of the grey thrushes. There was never a moment of quiet, and every moment the calls of five or more birds were superimposed upon one another. That was more than forty years ago, but the memory of it has the power to stir me even now.

Jackson left in December, with plans to return in the following spring. The year 1919 died hard. Its record shows that in our district it was the most disastrous of all years since the coming of the white man. The tally at Beaudesert Post Office shows that the rainfall of 1919 was lower even than that of 1902—Australia's worst drought year.

January 1920 brought a savage cyclone with heavy rain. Once more the ravines thundered to the voice of waterfalls. The face of the thirsty land changed almost overnight; within weeks grass was growing fence high throughout the district. The rainy season returned to its normal pattern, rounding off with light showers in May. Unseasonable winter rains brought early clover and the district faced one of the most promising springs in memory.

S. W. Jackson was due to return in the second week of September, and this time I was to be his camp mate. Herb had taken over the Kerry coach. Mick had been appointed ranger to Lamington National Park. Tom was away on a timber road job, and Ped, who returned from overseas in late 1919, was working in Lahey's huge sawmill in Canungra.

S. W. Jackson—1920 Camp

T EN days before Jackson was due to arrive, I went down with chills and fever, and spent my seventeenth birthday in bed with pleurisy, but I bounced back in time to help set up camp.

On this occasion Jackson travelled by hired car from Beaudesert to upper Kerry. Bill Rassmussen drove his car, a Maxwell Six, which was considered quite a car in those days. The naturalist did not come alone. Ernie Page, a young Hunter River man, had joined the expedition as an observer, at the instigation of R. H. Bettington, who was then at Oxford. A few years later, the name R. H. Bettington was familiar to many Australians as that of an international cricketer rather than an ornithologist; though the man was both. Ernie Page proved to be a likeable young man and a good camp mate. He was a better cook than I, though that could hardly be construed as praise.

For his second expedition, Jackson was desirous of establishing his headquarters as close as possible to the Antarctic beech forest. To this end his tents were set up in Norb's clearing beside the humpy. I occupied Norb's bunk in the humpy, and the two men had a tent each. We ate at a built-in table in the humpy and cooked at an open fireplace outside.

It was just over three years after Norbert's death in France, and there was much to remind me of him, even apart from the bunk which I occupied and the humpy, whose roofing iron had come eighteen miles by packhorse. There was the hard-won clearing, with its tall springboard stumps, which stood like towers above the high paspalum grass; across the gully, which cradles the infant Moran's Creek, was the orchard which Norb and Tom had planted. Those fruit trees had come by boat from Sydney, by train from Brisbane, by coach from Beaudesert, and by packhorse from Kerry, to the little clearing at the gateway to the Antarctic beech forest. Beside the humpy door, a rose, which Norb had planted, was in full bloom, and it was typical of S. W. Jackson that he photographed the rose and gave an enlargement to Mother.

After Norb's death his property passed to the family, but over twenty years later the land was resumed by the Government. These days much of Norb's clearing has been reclaimed by the forest, but present-day visitors to Green Muontains know it as the site of the forestry camp. The humpy stood just to the right, where the track first emerges into the clearing. Across the creek, where huts of the main camp now stand, you may still see three fruit trees—two peaches and a pear; they live on as memorials to Norb in his soldier's grave in France, and Tom, who lies in that lonely, empty land between the Mitchell and Palmer rivers of Cape York Peninsula.

The spring of 1920 was a different world from that of 1919. The moist winds blew across the range tops and we spent our days in a green land of mist and sunshine and bird calls, under the drip of the bearded trees. At evening, low clouds cascaded into the clearing, to mingle with the blue marara smoke of our camp fire, as the green catbirds cried their evening chorus. "Here I are" they cried, "Here I are."

The days and the weeks passed too swiftly for me; too swiftly for the ornithologist also. The birds' breeding season was well advanced and as yet there was no sign of nesting activity amongst the half-dozen pairs of atrichornis, whose habitats we had under observation. In desperation Jackson elected to return to Tom's Creek—a site which had been worked in the previous spring. Tom's Creek entered upper Moran's Creek from the east, after following a dark little gorge of its own making. It was a place of ferns and lofty trees, with great swinging loops of wisteria vines, and a spot beloved of the rufous scrub bird.

On the very first day our fortunes changed; we found a lone female and kept her under observation. She led us a merry dance under and around huge boulders, which overhung the little creek, through large areas of smashed cyclone debris, along the underside of logs and by other obstacles, to return after an hour to the starting point.

It seemed certain that there was a nest in the area, and it seemed equally certain that the lady was not going to lead us to it. Jackson discarded all attempts at stealth; he roughly outlined a circle of forest about a hundred yards in diameter and divided it into three segments—one for each of us to search.

It was my lot to find the nest; barely four feet above the water, on a perpendicular bank, and tucked knowingly under some small hanging fern. I called loudly that our quest was ended, and then I had an unpleasant second thought. Superficially the nest seemed identical with that of the white-browed scrub wren—that little scolding devil-bird, whose legions swarm the forest. Well, there was one way to find out. I put a finger through the neck of the nest and tapped a hard lining which gave off a hollow sound. My first guess had been right. Of all the birds of the world, there is but one which gives its nest a complete lining of water-proof hardboard made from wood pulp—that bird is atrichornis rufescens.

The nest yielded one hatched chick and one addled egg. That egg is the only one ever collected from an atrichornis in Queensland.

Around mid-December Jackson broke camp and once more the packhorses headed for the lowlands, with the naturalist's camp gear.

There are times when it seems that those three months of Jackson's 1920 camp had something to do with the shaping of my attitude towards life, and that somehow those days, under the ancient trees, are still with me. There was a quiet and a lack of urgency in the things we did together, the watching, learning and speaking in whispers, a sense of timelessness in the hours I spent alone, watching the nest-building of the olive whistler, the rufous fantail, the yellow robin, the dragoon bird. There was the return with Jackson and the camera to each nest, after the eggs were laid, and that night, under the glow of the ruby lamp, I saw the nest growing once more as the plate was developed. In the years since, it has seemed that the rush of life has always passed me by.

The Valley of Lost World

THERE would seem to be a contradiction involved in this book. So many pages were given over to Goblin Wood and the birds and the rains and the winds and the uneasy spirits of the rainforest.

Now I have left Goblin Wood and all the things which have been mine since 1917. Why does one leave paradise? Perhaps the answer lies somewhere in the earlier pages where I spoke of the challenge of the mountains. Green Mountains has imperishable beauty and a wonder that can never dim, but to me the challenge had gone. There is a road and a streamlined bus service, a big house with city amenities where a hundred gay, young city people may holiday at a time. There are splendid graded tracks through the forests, down the waterfall gorges and over the summits. Girls in high-heeled shoes, elderly ladies and gentlemen and couples with babies now stroll where but a few years ago only tough bushmen could go. The brushhook has been put away, the all-conquering axe has been relegated to the woodheap, the packhorse has been turned out for good; and up in Goblin Wood, the eager lad who had ridden up into the mountains in 1917 was now a middle-aged man who seemed to have outlived his times.

Nothing in life is static, we go forward or we slip back and as an eagle rises against the wind so, too, does man need adversity and challenge. More than that, I was one who had lost his dream, and he who loses his dream is already three parts dead in spirit. There were times at dawn or dusk or sometimes in the blue of a sapphire day when the smoky mists of a new dream would begin to crystallize into splendid colours . . . then they would fade with a disillusionment which had become habitual. But that was not the full story: I had returned from the war driven by a dangerous alcoholic problem. It is not my purpose here to go into first causes. The bodily chemistry and psychological propensities which render seven persons in every thousand susceptible to compulsive alcoholism are as yet imperfectly understood. Suffice it to say here that medical science now recognises compulsive alcoholism as one of the big four killer diseases of the Western world.

There is still, or course, some selfrighteous talk about weakness of will and defects of character of the alcoholic sufferers; this kind of outmoded thought belongs in the category which dismisses leprosy as a direct punishment of sin or which considers that an infant sufferer from a V.D. infection is being justly punished for the sin of an ancestor.

My drinking had roughly followed the pattern of many others whose indulgence had not led them to the final road of deadly compulsion—the difference was due in part both to the mysteries of biochemistry and psychological conditioning and, since there is evidence which tends to show that mental conditioning may influence bodily chemistry, the two are bound up together. When the point of no return has been reached a third factor enters the field—hopelessness. Medical science, which can give relief in almost every other field, has nothing to offer the compulsive alcoholic except the assurance that his condition will grow progressively worse.

To turn and start along the road back from a lost and hopeless position one needs the hand of God. Since all men are individuals the hand may not be the same to any two men; a man may not be aware of Whose hand he holds. An agnostic or an atheist sufferer may have another explanation or name for the phenomenon of his recovery—the name does not much matter since we are divided mainly by words. There are people outside the toils of the disease who think that a practising Christian should, purely by virtue of his faith, conquer alcoholic compulsion. That could be so if we possessed the faith of the saints and the martyrs, but we are everyday workers in an everyday world, not mystics of the cloister or the cave. To stand in the path of an on-coming train and depend on faith alone to keep one safe would be dangerous presumption. To suffer acute appendicitis and resort to faith alone instead of a good surgeon would be to fly in the face of God-given reason. Man, with his inherent intellect and freedom of will, is expected to find his way out of his own difficulties. The Lord is still on the side of those who help themselves—that seems to be part of the master plan.

In long and patient centuries of trial and error one problem after another has yielded to the probing minds of men and one dread disease after another has been tamed. So, too, the answer to chronic alcoholism has at last come up, but it contains no simple or dramatic remedy such as a drug or the surgeon's knife. Because of its very nature, the complex interplay of biochemical and psychological forces, the disease has no simple cureall, but the Key to complete and contented sobriety is to be found in an organization known as Alcoholics Anonymous. The word "Key" is here used in a literal sense—meaning that the sufferer on being given the Key must attend to his own unlocking.

My case might be taken as a classic example of how to bungle an unlocking. Too great an emphasis cannot be placed on the words "contented sobriety." It is easy to start off on the crest of enthusiasm which the first emancipation brings, but there is danger in this—there is a law that every wave crest is followed by a proportionately deep trough—we call it a let-down. When something which has dominated your life is suddenly removed, it leaves a dangerous vacuum; there is therefore a perilous period whilst a new way of life and thought and interest is being built up to fill the great void. This critical period is usually of nine months' duration—symbolical of the gestation period of human life is the period of an alcoholic's rebirth. Of all this I had been told by people who had found out—the hard way—had been told too that the best insurance against an early slip was group therapy—regular attendance at meetings. But of course, with the arrogance that is part of an alcoholic's makeup, I knew better. I was confident I was safe—nothing could happen to me now. A journey to Brisbane for a meeting meant the loss of a day and I couldn't afford to waste a day. The tragedy of it! A fool who had wasted years now couldn't spare days.

It was eight months before the inevitable crash came and then followed a period of despair which was just as unreasonable as the absurd overconfidence which had preceded it. Before, there was nothing that could harm me, afterwards there was nothing that could help me. A.A. would work for other people but my case was different. I went along to meetings, half-heartedly and with the preconceived idea that they would do me no good—naturally they didn't. I stumbled and picked myself up and tried half-heartedly again and again. I attended Mass and sometimes approached the Sacraments. I prayed spasmodically and without hope to a God Who I decided was leaving me as a deterrent to others. In all of this time the Key was within my grasp—yet eluded me; the mystic something which had been mine was no longer there. Nor can the why of it be fully explained. In all the trees of the vast forest of my home mountains you would not find two identical leaves though you searched for ever; a leaf is a simple thing compared to the complex mechanism of the human mind or the complex chemistry of the human body. It follows, then, that in any number of people with a common problem, each individual's problem is peculiarly his own and that the programme of A.A., which offers rehabilitation to all, must be all things to all men.

Those were the darkest days of my life and if there are still people in our midst who think that a compulsive alcoholic drinks because he likes to or wants to drink, let me tell them that had I the money of the Rockefellers at that time I would have traded it for peace and contented sobriety. Empty words! All the money in the world could not buy what I was seeking. I tried going away, taking jobs far afield—dazzled by the mirage of faraway places—strange mountains and green seas—magic lands where things would be different. But the world was not large enough and no man may escape himself though he travel to the moon. My attendances at meetings were without interest and far between, in fact they were kept up in an effort to convince my suffering family that I was trying to do something about my problem—a stratagem which deceived nobody.

It is difficult even with the wisdom of hindsight to attempt self-analysis over that period. It now has the smoky unreality of a horror dream. The one-time arrogance and rebellion of spirit had been drained away, but the tattered remnants of my Christian philosophy somehow supported my spirit—a moth fluttering feebly above the black bog of ultimate despair. But unknown to me, something was happening. My private Geth-semane was nearing an end and I still cannot tell you why. It is my belief that the prayers of my loved ones turned the scale; but to me prayer when answered is answered in a practical, working way.

Here were the things which appear to have been happening. The philosophy of A.A. absorbed during my "good" months was steadily nagging away at my subconscious. My meetings, futile as they appeared to be, were bringing me in touch with people who had made the grade after starting from positions far more hopeless than mine had seemed. I recall here a man holding down a position of trust as a caretaker—he had been a park metho-drinker four years earlier. There were men who had climbed to the very peak of their professions—the same men who, a few years earlier, had been unable to trust themselves to walk a hundred yards down Queen Street. The whole world seemed to be screaming, "They can do it, why can't you?" But it wasn't as simple as that—nothing in life ever is. I did not know the story or the agony which lay behind each recovery. Many speakers had told in general terms of their addiction and of the pattern of their recovery, but the true horror of an addict's world is so deep and secret that it cannot be communicated in words.

Then, too, there was the alcoholic's prayer which I had been repeating mechanically: "God grant me the serenity to accept the things I cannot change, courage to change the things I can, and the wisdom to know the difference." Well, I had accepted the fact that I was an alcoholic and that my life had become uncontrollable—so what? Did that make my lot any easier? I accepted, too, the fact that just one small glass of alcohol—that fatal first drink—would start the deadly chain reaction and wreck in one instant the little castle of hope built by the patient striving of months. But did that prevent me from taking it? But then there was the other part of the prayer "(give me) courage to change the things that can be changed." Here was something that was gnawing at me. What were the things that could be changed? Looming largest on the list was our family business set-up, a nightmare of joint ownership and divided control with its potential for stalemate and frustration: a difficult situation for a well-adjusted temperament, dynamite for mine. It was not within my power to change the set-up; the only possible change would have to come from me—get out and start something of my very own; but that was unthinkable. All that I owned and all that I hoped for were in the family show. With my sister Molly and brother Tom I had been part of it from the very first Easter party; with other members of my family I had worked without wages through eight dark depression years—all in the hope that some day things would come good, and now they were coming good.

More than once I had thought of breaking away—but man is tied strongly to his past. The happiness and the hardship and the hopes and the heartbreak of nearly forty years were tied up in Green Mountains and such property as I possessed was invested there also.

Viola and I were not young any more and for me the energy and enthusiasm of youth had been replaced by the sour wisdom and disillusionment of years and experience. It needed moral surgery of a major kind to cut Green Mountains out of my life and for a long time I hesitated. But whilst I was hesitating the years were marching. Still I paused in a haze of indecision, waiting for what? Perhaps for someone or something to give me a push, or perhaps I was waiting for a sign in the sky. However it may have been, it is true that the first sign did come from the sky. Unknown to us something awesome and terrible was building in the skies out above the waste of waters south of New Caledonia—the great killer cyclone of February 1954. It came like a homing rocket across a thousand miles of ocean, straight for Point Danger where the eastern end of our mountain range plunges into the sea, and thence the storm came inland along the backbone of our mountains, finally curving off to the south-east across the Tweed and the Richmond Valleys. As the "eye" of the storm crossed Point Danger the barometer dropped into the twenty-sevens in the lowest Australian reading since the Mackay cyclone of 1918. I was with a busload of passengers going up to Green Mountains when the first rush of the great wind caught us, about 10 p.m., in the rainforest nine miles from home. We reached home at dawn after leaving the stranded bus miles away. Somehow the snowstorm of flying branches and the eighty trees which fell across the road had left us unharmed. But, terrible as the wind was, the real horror was the rain. Thirty-eight to forty inches of rain fell in thirty-six hours. The Tweed and the Richmond Rivers, which caught the bulk of the run-off from our ranges, rose to unheard-of heights.

Through the afternoon and into the second night we listened to the eerie voice of radios sounding warning and doom—then Lismore's 2LM fell silent and we knew that the river city was under water. Alas, the early radio warnings were not heeded. When the floods went down twenty-eight dead were counted along the two rivers. After that storm things were never quite the same again. I went along the road in daylight and saw the countless tons of smashed timber. Then I thought of the twenty-eight dead, mostly farming people, family people—and I was still alive. What did it all mean? To me it meant that I had been given another chance—perhaps my very last chance.

There had been nothing within the memory of local people to parallel the magnitude of that storm. The main interstate railway which crossed the Macpherson Range west of Green Mountains was put out of commission for two months. The seventy odd miles of scenic tracks which were the key to the beauty of Lamington National Park were seventy miles of shattered rainforest debris, of landslides and rockfalls. In some places a hundred yards of track had disappeared without trace; in others, tree trunks had fallen across one another to make barriers up to twenty feet high all laced and tangled with water-vine and lawyer.

With the limited Forestry Vote available it would take years to repair the damage. (At the time of this writing after a lapse of eight and a half years, about 25 per cent of the tracks are still out of commission. In that time the rainforest with its magic has healed its own wounds, but the works of man have gone back to the wilderness.) However, extra men were put on to begin the huge job of clearing and I jumped at the opportunity of joining them. It was good clean man's work under the big trees, with keen axe, saw and brush-hook; the great red chips of scented timber; and the axe blows echoing across the ranges. There was deep satisfaction, too, in the knowledge that we were working to restore to the people the beauty that was lost to them. Those were good days, good nights too, under canvas in our camp at Nixon's Creek—the red galley fire, the voice of an adolescent waterfall and the night wind in the giant messmates above, the dingo howl, the scream of the winking owl, the cosy voice of the mopoke and sleep, blessed sleep.

Each Friday after knock-off time I walked twelve miles home round by the border ramparts, and on each Sunday walked back to camp. This was a wet or fine routine. Had I believed in luck, I would have thought myself lucky that my tent mate should have been Roger, but by this time a certain pattern seemed to be taking shape and things were beginning to fall into place. Roger, a lean, silver-haired veteran of Gallipoli and France, looked what he was, soldier, horseman, bushman and gentleman. But of even more importance to me in the companionship of this well-spoken enlightened man was the fact that he, too, had a problem and his problem was my problem. In this we shared a deep, unspoken fellowship wherein each was aware of the other's trouble and without ever approaching the matter in direct words each was able to supply the other with missing pieces of the jig-saw puzzle. Philosophies and personalities, rubbing together constantly for months, somehow worked their own queer brand of magic and I am happy to report that the years that have gone since those days on Nixon's Creek have been years of continuous and contented sobriety for Roger, even as they have been for me.

During that autumn and winter my life slipped into quiet waters. No longer mine to make decisions, my days and nights were ordered for me; no need to think, the present was provided for, the past was gone, the future had not yet come—my job, my tent and the galley fire, the week-end walk to Green Mountains and a little serious reading. What did these add up to? Something that fell a little short of living. There was still my old love— the rainforest and its people, life under the big trees, but I'd always had that and it hadn't always been enough. Money? No, there was ample for my needs—strangely, though, I still bought an occasional Golden Casket ticket knowing as I did so that a big win would have given me the ready means for my swift and total destruction. At times, too, there were thoughts of a car—but to what purpose? To smash up myself or others. No; the quiet backwater for me—but could that be all? There was still that urge to write, an urge temporarily satisfied in the writing of verse scraps—mostly unfinished. But it was that same urge which had spelt heartbreak and wasted months a short year before. After the moderate success of my other books it was easy for me to argue that people with a gift of expression have a duty to the world, but my writing while satisfying in places had become hopelessly patchy and seemed to have lost its purpose, quite logically, since the author had lost his. No; writing was out. "I will go quietly through my years." There was a sad negative ring about that, but there seemed to be no choice. Somewhere past midwinter came the first danger signs, boredom and restlessness. To what extent the symptoms might have developed is not known because relief came swiftly and from an unexpected quarter. Never was a blessing more thoroughly disguised than the big July cyclone of 1954. The challenge of weather at its worst touches something elemental in the soul of man; something from the morning of time was in that little camp under the giant messmates, in the rain-lashed galley with its smoky fire, in the thunder of the great wind and the crack and crash of timber. The age-old challenge to survival, where life was a battle and not a quiet asylum, was somehow hammering out the answer I sought.

On the heels of the July cyclone came brilliant skies and roaring waterfalls. At long last the season levelled out into typical Queensland weather—that cloudless weather which can be the loveliest on earth. Blue day followed blue day around the corner and into spring; wild flowers came alive along the Ship's Stern track and the rufous fantails returned from the Indies; everywhere orchids were blooming and birds were building. Life in the mountains was quickening and something was happening to me. Looking back from this distance it would seem that the answer was purpose—that life to have meaning cannot be negative. It meant, too, that I must change my way of life again. There was something else too; as August turned to September something else came, something that I had been without for so long—something that I had never thought to hold again—that most blessed of all things—hope. There is a theory of action and reaction which postulates that because the universe exerts its effect on a creature, that creature must in some small way affect the universe. Certainly time and space were working for me: in the time of the flowers and the birdnesting, hope had come back; back, when the rufous fantails were returning across the Arafura Sea; and from the breeding ground of the great black storms far out in the Coral Sea a purpose in life had ridden in on the very wings of the big wind.

In a Readers' Digest I had read and pondered the six words of Chinese philosophy, "It is later than you think." Yes, it was late—perhaps too late. I walked along the forestry track and looked out across my ranges, pale blue with smoke haze. I breathed the scent of orchids and distant burning gumleaves. Here were the things I loved and here was security. What was wrong with me? Nothing, save that I didn't want that kind of security. I wanted to dream again and follow my dream in a new land of trackless forests and unnamed waterfalls. I wanted a chance to start again as I had started in 1917 and a chance to recapture the days when the world was wide and wonderful. Just a dream, but the whole structure of happiness is built upon dreams; a lover dreams of love, a millionaire dreams of more millions and I dreamed of enchanted forests and eternal youth.

Goblin Wood with its joys and sorrows was tied to me like a stone around my neck, but all of its cords were from the past and the past was gone beyond recall. Why wait on the future? The future belonged in another dimension but the present was mine. The present is all that we ever have in which to accomplish anything. The past is a haunting ghost; the future a vague cloud spectre in the distant sky—the to-morrow that never comes. To-day—now! That is the time for action. I went back to Goblin Wood and packed a few things into a couple of bags. The daffodils and the azaleas were blooming and a grey thrush was singing in the treefern outside Rhelma's window as I walked down the path to the bus without looking back. That is important; when you make up your mind don't look back.

Once before I had gone off and left Goblin Wood—that was when I was going to war, and I looked back a last time and hoped some day to return: but this time there was to be no looking back, nor turning back. My journey was to be a long one—not in miles but in time. He who tries to put back the clock has far to go and he who would journey back in the fourth dimension must travel beyond the stars. But in the geographical sense my journey was not far. Along towards the south-west, beyond the far cliffs of Lost World Plateau, where the sabre of time has slashed deep into the green heart of the ranges, is the walled gorge which we have called the Valley of Lost World. It is a land where great mountains leap and fall in static rhythm—a land of great forests dark in mystery. Remote enough for him who seeks the wilderness for its own sake, its approach is none the less easy. In a short two hours from Brisbane you may stop your car by the river under the giant cliffs of Lost World. If you follow the road on up the Albert

River past Kerry and through Darlington you will come at last to the land where the great rainforest once stood, where the Stephens and the Keaveney men moved in with their axes and their spring-boards a short generation ago. You will pass the big homes of the Stephens men and you will see some of the finest bullocks in all the land, grazing where the great stands of hoop pine and silky oak had darkened the ridges within my memory. And beyond all this you will see mountains so splendid that they will dim your eyes. And if you go on past the last of the works of man to the edge of the forest where great basalt mountains tower and a wild river runs between, then you are on the threshold of the Valley of the Lost World. It was here across the river from where the timber begins that I raised my little roof; for my new dream had a name and its name was "The Valley of Lost World."

As far back as 1947 I had planned a stopover tourist cabin in the valley—little more than a shelter which would enable walking or riding parties to visit the western area of Lamington National Park. Th scheme got as far as the purchase and partial erection of two used pre-fabricated army huts; but the fierce rains and winds of that season plus my lack of steadfast purpose had wrecked the venture before it was fairly started. Now I was going to start again, but this time it was planned to erect permanent buildings—a bit at a time—and to coax people into my new country. I had been associated with the tourist industry for nearly thirty years; it was the only thing I knew anything about and it was rather late to teach an old dog new tricks.

On a broad bench forty feet above the river was a little 12ft. × 12ft. army humpy with galvanized iron roof and walls and a concrete floor. Alongside was a broad rectangle of concrete floor, all that remained of a kitchen which had been spread over the landscape in the savage winter cyclone of 1950. This had been a wartime feeding point; a place where the boys could get their first hot meal after days of hard rations on manoeuvres in the Macpherson rainforests—a tough apprenticeship for a grim trade.

There had also been a little casualty station sited in that quaint way which the army had, on the opposite side of the river so that in flood time it was cut off from the kitchen. I walked into the humpy; here was home—until my new roof was raised. The open doorway (the door and the windows had long since gone) looked downriver to the west, down across the rich bright green of clustering second-growth trees, all restless in the valley breeze. From the window one looked up the gorge directly on to noisy river rapids where the water, marbled green and white, rushed from under the overhang of the rainforest. Behind loomed the great dark mountains, trackless and unspoiled as in the days before Captain Cook—an enchanted land.

Fifty yards away and almost completely hidden by a giant purple bougainvillea was a beekeeper's cottage, now deserted. Built before the days of petrol pumps, its walls were shingled with flattened petrol tins—in its early days the cottage had supported the bougainvillea and it was good to see the vine now supporting the cottage in its tottering old age. Not far away was a lone and lichen-covered post leaning out of line—all that remained of a selector's humpy. The lad who built it, Alf. Stephens, found a soldier's grave in France in 1917. I like to think of that post and the stones of his fireplace as Alf's memorial rather than the honour stones which bear his name, just as my brother Norb's true memorial is a tiny clearing high on Green Mountains and a hardy fruit tree which came eighteen miles by packhorse so long ago.

There was a half-hearted attempt to set up my housekeeping things in the humpy, but the river gorge was calling. I dropped everything and went almost running beside the leaping water along its obstacle course strewn with great blocks of red lava—on until the rainforest met overhead. I was naming things as I went, green pools and monoliths and gateways of rock: "Big Brother," "Flooded Cavern," "Pine Tower," "Jade Pool," "Lava Pool," "Jotun's Gateway," "The Rocks of the Moon," "The Pool of the Feathered Serpent." The latter was abutted by a rock formation suggestive of a ruined Maya temple so that the fanciful name was not inappropriate. It was in mild delirium that I followed the gorge—this was my country, my new country—and this was my new life. I had been given another start—a chance to begin again. It was as though I had passed through an interminable black night of delirium and horror and had awakened to a glorious morning of spring flowers and singing birds. Gone were the black mists of frustration and hopelessness and despair, blown away in the clean wind that rushed down the gorge from the high country beyond; swept away in the green, rushing waters of my wild and lovely river. But afar a faint note of warning sounded through this intoxication of mood—the hard-earned lesson that intoxication must bring its hangover.

The gold of evening was on the cliffs when I returned to the humpy, fresh from a swim in the lava pool and the cold clean bite of mountain water. Twigs from a tallow-wood tree and then a fire, thick rump steak in the pan and a billy of tea and then the stars.

The wire stretcher-bed was set up and for my pressure lantern a bedside table was rigged from the box section of an old hive left by the beekeeper, John Rosser. There was a mosquito net, but it remained folded as a second pillow; swift running water and a restless river wind left no breeding or hovering places for the little pests. With awakening excitement a new geology book was unwrapped from bookseller's paper. This, too, was part of the plan. From its birthplace on Mount Throakban, the Rainmaker, to the rapids below the window, my river had lain bare the bones of the mountains on whose doorstep I had come to live; they were to be my immediate and intimate neighbours and it was my wish to know them better. Now the new book would help me follow their story graven in rock to be read down the ages.

Presently winged people of the forest and the night came along to pay court to my three hundred candlepower light—pathetic moths and pestiferous borers and other annoying wogs. The moths I escorted outside behind the dark of the bougainvillea, but the others were making themselves offensive around the floor when there was a soothing, gliding sound and two feet of beautiful banded black and white Bandi Bandi snake slithered from a crack in the concrete by the wall and set about having supper off my unwelcome visitors. Bandi Bandi snakes are venomous, but are very well mannered and mind their own business. An unregistered partnership came into being right away—I was to supply the lamp which attracted the snake's food, the snake on his part agreed to rid me of my annoying wogs—and so our friendship prospered during my weeks in the old humpy; to the best of my belief he is still there. This, then, was the new order, the voice of the rapids and the river wind, the black mountains, the white stars—and the snake; I turned out the lamp and drifted into nine hours of untroubled sleep.

New day came in bright-coloured wrappings and an airy damask of mist on the high table of Lost World; my table down below was more humble as befitting one who eats below the salt, my damask a two-day-old newspaper; but the chorus of the magpie minstrel and the woodwind of the black and white butcher-birds were for all.

My mood was still far from normal; the bubble of adventure, the joy of emancipation and the wild splendour of the mountains had combined to render me more unstable emotionally than usual. It was a very pleasant form of unreality and it was good to enjoy it whilst I might, for I knew that reality was waiting for me and that hard facts were piled up ahead like stones in a pyramid. Still, there was a light-hearted almost innocent approach and it appears now from this distance that the innocence and light-heartedness were a gift of God, for without them I could never have faced up to the new order and without the new order the black horror of my illness might not have been driven from my life.

My innocence—I could never call it audacity— is laughable now. I had £200 in the bank, no job and no income, no property in my own name on which I could raise money. The barest essentials in building and plant necessary for my new business would have cost around £3,000. And even if I could have spent that amount, there would still have been no business. The big business connections at Green Mountains had been built up slowly over the years, mainly by personal recommendation. The Green Mountains house was a going concern with a bus service from Brisbane and was the hub of a network of splendid tourist tracks radiating through Lamington National Park. My plant at this stage was an axe—my own—a bar, shovel and crosscut saw borrowed from brother Herb; just these under the cedar trees in a wild valley that no one had ever heard of. All this, just seven weeks to Christmas when it was planned to coax my first tourists into the Valley of Lost World! Add to this the fact that it was planned to do my own building to conserve funds. Oh yes, I'd done some building in the early days of Green Mountains, but again merciful Providence and the years had veiled the fact that such building was as offsider to a carpenter who did the measuring, cut the bevels and said, "Do this, do that." Oh yes, over in the humpy beside the geology book was yet another book, "Ye Compleat Carpenter," a tome crammed with information and diagrams which in theory enabled the reader to build anything from a dog kennel to a parish hall. Oh innocence—with the good book in one hand and the good hammer—not yet bought—in the other, I was going to build me a house and in record time, too.

Over under the cedars where the first unit of the house was to go I found near-forgotten relics of my stillborn venture of 1947; well, that was water under the bridge, this was 1954 or what was left of it. Mistakes can be valuable if you try to profit by them; almost the whole edifice of human progress has been built upon the heartbreaking foundations of trial and error. The cedars were low and limby and clustered around the home site. Here a bare thirty-five years ago noble rainforest had stood to a height of two-hundred feet—now it was grassed up to the National Park boundary across the river and dotted with lovely trees, secondary growth from the original forest, red cedar, white cedar, silky oak, black bean, rose mahogany, tamarind, hoop pine and Moreton Bay fig. But in that fine litany of names it was the red cedar which captured the imaginaton—red cedar, that fabulous timber whose very name was magic in the last century. Unlike most Australian trees red cedar is deciduous—in this it commends itself as a house tree as its handsome leaves which give shade in the heat of the year are shed to let in the winter sun; add to this the beauty of its gold in autumn and the red splendour of its newborn leaves of spring. The name cedar is a misnomer: the tree is the well-known cedrela toona of India and persists through Malaya, Indonesia, New Guinea and down Australia's east coast far into New South Wales.

Well, there it was—a bar and shovel and matted Kikuyu grass waist deep; a hot November sun and three-score of inquisitive Hereford bullocks drawn up in crescent formation. Every time I threw down the shovel they broke formation and galloped away, only to re-form and come galloping back. These were Stephens bullocks and as though there wasn't sufficient "sidewalk supervision" on my side of the fence there was an equal number of "supervisors" on the Keaveney side. These were led by a supercilious-looking, wide-horned red which I dubbed Pieface. Every time I stopped to wipe the sweat out of my eyes Pieface would shake his head with a pitying look of "You poor bloody fool, what do you think you are doing there?" What indeed! If I could have thought of an answer I'd have told him. It was when trying to measure and square the pegs for the foundation stumpholes that I was to find out how muddled and uncertain was my concentration. In overeagerness to get everything exact, half-a-dozen sets of calculations would be made—with half-a-dozen different results. At screaming point I would look up to see Pieface licking his lips with a look of "It won't be long now."

"Damn and blast you" I'd yell, bouncing a stone off his ribs, "I'll be here when you've gone to the meatworks"; but that outburst was only meant to reassure myself.

Towards evening there was the sound of a heavy truck coming up the flat by the Lake of the Two Ducks. Lloyd Timms, the Darlington carrier, was bringing my sawn hardwood. Presently the green Bedford came nosing its way through the cedars. We unloaded the timber in the last light before an interested group of spectators; a couple of hundred white faces ringed us in the dusk. My thought at the time was, "If only a few of the higher animals would take a similar interest in my venture."

The tools had arrived and the nails. There were sufficient foundation stumps to allow the laying of some of the bearers. The sensible thing, of course, would have been to put down all the stumps first, but I was sick of bar and shovel, I wanted to get on with the sawn timber—to see how good I was. What a waste of time! A little thought and a little memory would have served to tell me that I was useless with sawn timber—always had been, always would be.

It took me more than a week to acknowledge what I already knew—that the job was beyond me. Then, with a little over five weeks to my deadline, I went rushing off in search of a tradesman. It seemed to me that there should have been a whole row of carpenters standing waiting to be asked so that they could rush out and do my job . . . it was a shock then to find that none was available until after Christmas. That did it. I went back to Lost World with my barometer at dead low. The whole idea had been crazy; I'd get out and leave. No I wouldn't, I'd take a job and then come back in the New Year. Yes, I would; no, I wouldn't. My teacup storm raged by the campfire and never did the mountains and the stars seem more aloof from me and my petty troubles—"This is your show, don't look to us for help" they seemed to say.

Then I remembered with relief that Viola and Rhelma were going to Coolangatta for a holiday and, though my time was running out and my money close behind it, I deemed it my business to see them off in Brisbane. My real business was to escape the tension and indecision which had built up in the valley. My family went off to the coast on Saturday morning; I had thought of putting off my return to the valley until after the week-end, but recognising fatal symptoms in that postponement, had booked a seat on the Beaudesert Saturday morning bus. However, for some reason which I tried to tell myself was accidental I walked into the Greyhound Depot ten minutes after the bus had gone. A few minutes later I was back in my hotel dining-room ordering yet another pot of strong tea—they thought me mad—maybe I was.

Across in town my wanderings reflected those of my mind. First, up the marble steps of the Treasury Building to the showroom of the Mines Department, there to spend an hour amongst showcases which glittered with the spoils of Queensland's rich mineral and gem fields. Deliberately I dazzled my eyes with those two powerful mirages which have ever led men from their firesides—the vision of buried treasure and the call of faraway places. I felt the pull of the magnet which took brother Tom from his home mountains to that far country of sudden riches and sudden death—to that loneliest of graves beyond the Mitchell River.

I wandered along Queen Street, my head full of the blue sapphires of Anakie and the black opals of Eromanga. Presently, without quite knowing why, I was in the Moreton Galleries. Host James Wieneke was conversing with some earnest-looking people and I went around alone amongst landscapes of smoky blue, of purple mountains and desert reds—faraway places again. From there my erratic trail led to a picture theatre which I left after fifteen minutes, and finally across Elizabeth Street to St. Stephen's Cathedral. Here was peace—not the peace which I was seeking, that of a settled mind which knows where it is going—this was the peace of another world, the timeless peace of the cloister, echoing footsteps in the pillared gloom, the highlights of stained-glass windows, the live ruby heart of the sanctuary lamp. But, with me, the peace of God belongs in His house; when I go out once more into the land of bread and butter it is left behind, though I feel that the nearest one may come to true peace in this world is to lie in the doorway of the next. But the cloister was not for me; outside in the world of people and everyday things my battle must be fought. Presently the cathedral echoed to many sounds as a wedding party came up to the altar rails. The very domesticity of the scene jarred me— it was as though a housewife with a pudding bowl had walked between me and my Creator. I left the cathedral in a huff.

Afternoon found me at the Exhibition Building, brushing through modern English watercolours with mounting irritation. It was bad enough, I thought, when the patent-medicine people used irritation tactics to sell their wares—now the artists were doing it. My last call for the day was to the Museum where I was caught up with rock fossils until closing time. Here was the past. The weird little trilobites of the Cambrian rocks, outlandish little horrors from the far-off morning of the world, were here to remind me that my life with all its problems, real and imaginary, was as less than a flash of lightning in the long, dark night of Time. Next morning I came from early Mass bubbling over with the joy of living. Had I resolved my problems? Of course not—just postponed them for yet another day whilst I went to Coolangatta to spend the Sunday with my family. By contrast with the previous morning I was at the bus depot forty-five minutes before departure time.

The trip to the coast was not wasted. As we put the smooth miles of Pacific Highway behind us I was getting far enough away from the valley to take an objective view of things and to work out a plan of action for the future. The plan was to work and to save money until February, then return to the valley with carpenters and build the first section of Lost World House in time to open for Easter 1955. That plan, once formed, was adhered to—there was to be no turning back; even if it was going to be a big mistake, go ahead and make it— no more indecision. But first it was decided that a visit to my repatriation doctor would be wise. The doctor, who found me tightly strung and over-excited, put me in a hospital bed and gave me a course of needles. A few days later I walked out, as steady as a church and at peace with the world.

The big Christmas and New Year season at Green Mountains was at hand . . . extra help was needed, so I returned to the old address and worked through until the last week in January.

It was time for me to go back to the valley. February had come, but so had the big rains; already one cyclone had side-swiped the Queens-land coast and the gorges were roaring with white water. My river ford, two miles down from the building site, was washed out and boulder-strewn: anyhow, it was still too deep for a vehicle. This, it seemed, was going to be just another of those super wets.

There was a local building boom and my carpenters, Keith and George, couldn't sit around waiting for my weather to turn fair and my river to go down—they had other commitments—but they agreed to come out at week-ends and get my job under way, if, or when, things cleared up around Lost World.

Things did. The sun shone hot and steamily, the river fell, the Shire Council men repaired the crossing. Keith and George were to make a dawn start from Beaudesert on Saturday, the first unit of Lost World house would soon be under way—or would it? Keith's big red truck chose that Saturday dawn to get into the act. Somewhere after noon they got her started and somewhere after 1 p.m. they turned up at Lost World wishing that it had stayed lost.

From there on to the end of the job we had a rainmaking formula which left the C.S.I.R.O. and the witch-doctors for dead. As the first hammer blows echoed among the crags of Lost World the first drops of rain began to fall and as the tempo of the hammering increased so did the tempo of the rain. The carpenters worked hard in the wet—

doubtless in the spirit that the sooner the job was finished the sooner they'd be done with the place.

It was a small rain depression which had moved in that week-end. Before long the river began to get noisy and white and Keith decided to go, but the red truck had other ideas, backed up by wet wiring and a low battery. I legged it across the river a mile downstream to my nearest neighbour, Graham Stephens. Graham said, "Sick bomb, eh," climbed on to his tractor with a spare battery and drove to the rescue. Red truck and tractor soon moved off down the road ahead of the fast-rising water.

Sometimes now I wonder if the venture would ever have got going without Graham and his help—and his telephone. With the carpenters safely back in Beaudesert the rain stopped like magic, but that week-end performance, apart from the temperamental truck, was repeated so often that we lost count.

There was another complication which was to lose us precious time. A ton of roofing iron had been ordered in Brisbane some time before. The building framework had been completed under unusual difficulty and all was ready for the roof; but where was the iron? Once more Graham's 'phone ran hot whilst I cranked its handle. The merchants had dispatched it a fortnight ago. The carriers had not received it. I thought of hijackers; but finally the mystery was solved—the iron had been sent to Canungra by mistake. "Sorry," and all that. I had been sitting at Lost World, the carpenters had been sitting in Beaudesert, and the iron had been sitting in Canungra all through a fine week-end (the only fine week-end), and all the time the clock was ticking away the hours to Easter.

The t-and-g floors could not be laid before the roof was on and then there was a little mountain of stuff in Beaudesert; furniture and furnishings, bedding, kitchen-ware, dining-ware, stove, refrigerator, all waiting for the roof—and the river. We were expecting seven guests for Easter and I am still wondering what those people would have thought had they known that, with a bare three weeks to go, Lost World house was a roof-less timber skeleton under the cedars.

Next week-end the roofing-iron came, so did Keith and George, so did the rain but the roof went on and at last there was some shelter for indoor work. In a few days that followed the flats dried up and Lloyd, with his Bedford, brought our mountain of gear from Beaudesert. Well for us that he took advantage of that opportunity—it was to be the last. Unknown to us, a lady was about to take a hand in the game, a lady who for a few short days would wield more power than Catherine of Russia—a lady named Bertha.

Bertha

YOU read much of the horror and the devastation of cyclones, but seldom anything to their credit. The big rains which attend them may bring widespread benefit to the land, but this is often offset by wind damage, flooding and the waterlogging of pastures. It is not an unusual thing in these latitudes for a three-day spinning storm to yield up to thirty inches of rain, the bulk of which may fall in a grand, final burst. To the mountain man the cyclone brings drama on a mammoth scale—the splendour of the piling clouds when big weather is making in the black mountains, the ropes of white vapour sucked by the rushing updraughts through cliff chimneys, the mighty roar of the wind mounting in power, gust by gust, when a million trees take up its song as it funnels through the gorges, the wild screaming flight of the birds, and the white walls of rain that come with the pressure of a fire hose. Then between the gusts comes another sound, low and grumbling at first, then rising and full of menace as torrents begin to speak.

Cyclone Bertha, the second of the 1955 cyclone season, had an unheralded beginning and approach. She spawned in the East Coral Sea far away from the air routes and the steamer lanes and came undetected almost to our doorstep. Friday had been gusty with splendid clouds pushing up from behind Mt. Worendo and sailing down the sky over Lost World, their dark-blue shadows deepening the dark of the rainforest. They looked just what they were, proud outriders of a great storm.

There was a subtle something in the wind and in the arrogant sweep of the clouds which seemed to give a hint of bigger things, but the radio at Graham's had words only for a high pressure system in the Tasman, "fresh winds and isolated showers along the coast." Twice in the night rain blew lightly across me through the open window and a dawn squall caught me in the frying of bacon and eggs—rain sizzled into the pan and the fire. The weather looked wild at the head of the gorge, but the sun came hot and bright between squalls. Keith and George came early and started on the floor and the walls.

"Business as usual," Keith remarked, ducking out of a shower. "Brought the casements for the corner and the sills for them," he added. At last! The six windows which were to frame the crag of

Mt. Widgee. I opened them up and gave a yelp like a kicked pup.

"Arctic glass! How the hell are you going to see Mt. Widgee through arctic glass?"

"Must have made a mistake," conceded Keith. Once more I was cranking Graham's 'phone.

"Yes, clear-glass casements; we have 'em—you can send the others back."

"Get 'em on Bob Johnston's truck today?"

"I'll try."

At all costs I wanted those casements in position when Viola and Rhelma arrived. But I could have saved myself the trouble—it was not to be. Over the skyline around the curve of the earth a little north of east was Bertha—undreamed of alike by weather men and laymen—Bertha with her head down, running full tilt at the Queensland coast, her wet cloud-pigtails whipping.

Through the day the weather seemed to hold down to a norm, neither wet nor dry, but the clouds were piling and stirring in a foreboding way. White masses came rushing low round the black crag of Widgee to be caught in a sucking draught which drew them suddenly up thousands of feet to join the turbulent banks above—a force vast and invisible was beginning to pull the strings.

In an afternoon lull I brought over tucker and the lantern from the humpy. Our new building was to have tenants for the first time. There was a roof and an L of wall to the east and the north. Keith nailed roofing iron over the staring window-ways and it would have been quite cosy in any but cyclone weather. Like a long low haystack down the centre were the big piles of mattresses, pillows and cosy quilts in big bundles corded in tarred paper. We tore some of them open and got bedding for three, and we fished out three wire stretchers from under the house; here was luxury. It was different from the way I'd planned my first night in the new building. There was uneasiness about the weather, the future, the river, the road, the first guests. A bright new "Saturday Evening Post," still smelling of Philadelphia, failed to hold my attention and presently with the light out, listening to the intermittent showers on the new roof and the big drops blown from the red cedars, I was thinking "This is what I wanted to hear, the rain on my own new roof"; but the thought brought only anxiety. Presently I slept, vaguely conscious of freshening wind and of heavier rain on the roof.

By morning the showers were beginning to merge into one, but, as yet, not heavy enough to cause alarm—or so I thought. The men had indoors work to do and so the only real problem was the cooking of breakfast which I finally managed under a couple of sheets of roofing iron leant against a cockspur bush.

Somehow I'd been reckoning without the rain which is always a great deal heavier on the high border country. All night it must have been roaring down on that high land of cloud and moss, because when I strolled casually down to the crossing on my way to the hut, after breakfast, the river was a brown torrent, thigh deep and thick with drift. It scared me but I went in—the river plucked at my legs but my heavy boots and heavy weight kept me upright. A quick dash to the hut where I scooped up half a tin of kerosene and four pounds of corned beef and was back at the river within five minutes, but it was deeper and making angry sounds. Lifting my feet wasn't safe so I shuffled, body bent upstream whilst the river sucked stone and gravel from under my boots. The bank was a welcome sight. Dumping my burden I ran to the building yelling to the men "Go for your lives!" and then dragged open the gate for them. Keith and George piled into the truck and proceeded to carry out my advice. The lower crossing was shallow and wide and two miles downstream, but the flood was going like a trotting pony. As it was, they only just made it; their truck stalled in the crossing but they got it going again—otherwise it might have finished up in Moreton Bay. I turned back to the river bank to retrieve my meat and kerosene. It had only been about ten minutes, but in that time the flood had risen the best part of a foot. By now the wind was at what the weather men call gale force, and the rain beating out a steady inch an hour—"even time" rain, twenty-four inches in twenty-four hours, is not uncommon in these storms.

I got the little woodstove inside by sliding it up a plank—then I got a fire going in it and put my corned beef on to boil in a big billycan. The next item was to erect a temporary wall along the wall-less lee side of the main wing; this was done with eight-foot sheets of roofing iron. There was a difficulty in this, the iron could not be nailed in place without spoiling it for its ultimate use. It was held in place by barricades of stretcher beds and cleats of sawn hardwood, but the whole structure was as temporary as it sounds and needed a constant watch and some fixing from time to time. It stood well in the gusts, but tended to suck back into the room in the back draughts.

By mid-afternoon the voice of the river began to mingle with the roar of the wind and the rain, and the toss of its tawny mane flashed high above the banks from time to time. Things were happening down there, so down I went in bathing trunks and with a wet cornbag to take the sting of the rain from my shoulders. In my time I've seen big rivers in big flood, and they were rather like the tide of Tennyson, "too full for sound," but this was the wildest thing I'd ever seen.

The river here has a bed about fifty yards wide, is almost devoid of gravel, and is composed mostly of blocks of lava ranging from the size of a football to the size of a week-end cottage, and apart from a pool every 400 yards or so it is white water all the way. Now it was filled brimful with roaring, racing water, mad water that was leaping ten feet in white anger; mangling, crushing water that was rolling and grinding rocks as big as wool bales down its turbulent bed. Perhaps the most lasting impression was one of naked, primitive power—the elemental power that tears down mountains and fills ocean beds.

With dusk came a feeling of infinite loneliness; the storm and the high river had cut me off from my fellow men, and just for a little while I felt like the last man alive in a world that was tearing itself to pieces. A meal, a few final touches to the temporary wall and then the night, the long black night so full of noise and violence. No place was quite dry; misty spray drifted everywhere and into everything, but it was warm, almost hot, and there was no personal discomfort.

I opened the "Saturday Evening Post" at a colour picture—red desert mountains washed by the Arizona sun, and wished myself there. The wind was still rising and maul-like blows on the east side made me thankful for the stout ironbark timbers between me and the storm. The temporary wall, though on the lee side, needed fairly frequent attention.

I was dozing with the lantern turned down when sheets of iron tore loose from a window-way. After ten minutes of wrestling with the iron in the windy dark they were cleated back into position. I stepped out of my soaking clothes and left them outside where they lay.

During another doze, part of the temporary wall blew in across me and a four by two of hardwood nearly broke my wrist; another ten minutes of wrestling from the inside and some kind of order was restored. This time there was a vow that there would be no more dozing until things were quieter.

This was a queer night; different again from the many nights I'd ridden cyclones out in the old humpy on Moran's Creek, at Goblin Wood, in the galley on Nixon's Creek with the big messmates bending and threshing overhead, or the wild night on Stockyard Creek Divide with my back to a tallow-wood tree and a bottle of rum in my pocket—that, at least, was one bottle of rum I have never begrudged myself.

This night was indescribably dark; a four-mile depth of black stormcloud was superimposed on the normal black night of the gorge. The mingling thunders of rain, wind and river, the shivering shocks of the gusts, the bumping, thudding vibration of big rocks grinding down the riverway before the appalling force of the water—these were the sounds and the sensations which filled my whole world. Sometimes I had the feeling that, out in the darkness, the mountain which towered from my doorstep to the sky was crumbling and that I was listening to its death agony.

Then there came another sound, more disquietening than the booming night outside—a loud singing in my ears. In a cyclone you only hear that sound when the air pressure falls to danger level—it is the death song of the Yellow Sea and the Caribbean. There was a short period of violent wind, then a calm, after which the wind suddenly wheeled more than 90 degrees. Slowly my head cleared of its singing and slowly the wind and the rain began to die.

The clock showed less than an hour to dawn and the gusts were losing their power. There were lengthening lulls between downpours and the rain itself became lighter with each squall. But now, as the sounds of the wind and the rain ceased, the full anger of the river filled the wild pre-dawn with its booming, grinding and thudding.

Somehow the little stove was relit, the lantern light was fluttering in the dying wet gusts, and presently there was a billy of strong tea with much sugar. The corned beef yielded to a fork—it was cooked, there was bread and butter; this then was breakfast and as it progressed light began to show through the cedars; the long dark night was over. Not a night of terror but one of uneasiness and E-string tension, and crashing with Wagnerian overtones.

Once more the sun came hot and bright and the cliffs above were shedding their water. Bertha herself was not such a big noise as cyclones go, but she had partly wrecked a little town north of Brisbane and had made a sizeable hole in my plans. The radio people, who in the first place hadn't noticed Bertha until she was trying to blow down their aerials, now assured us that the unruly lady had gone out to sea off Point Danger—and so she had, but it wasn't goodbye, it was au revoir. For a week she roamed the wastes of the North Tasman and then the squeeze of a high-pressure system forced her back once more along the familiar track to Point Danger.

Blissfully unaware of all this I began to rearrange my plans. In the meantime there were the airing and drying of anything damp—and that meant everything. The rain had stopped at dawn on Monday. Viola and the Imp were to arrive on Friday and our first Easter guests on the following Thursday night. As yet fewer than half the walls were up and none of the partitions, doors or windows; the stretcher beds, which had no legs, had to be built on to the walls in double-deck, ship's cabin style.

By Tuesday afternoon I was able to ford the river in quiet water at the foot of a waterhole below Graham's pumphouse. The water was strong and waist deep, but I used a light pole to prop myself. There had been no bridge damage downstream, but all approach cuttings had been filled with black silt. Graham, with a grader-blade on his tractor, had been clearing silt from bridge decks and approaches. The road was clear, then, as far as my crossing-place and all was ready for our Easter party except that the house was only half built. "The floods are in the ocean, the stream is clear again" Henry Lawson sang—now I could only hope that the skies would keep clear and let our carpenters come back at the week-end. In the meantime my only vehicular crossing, two miles away, was thigh deep and paved with loose melon-sized rocks.

On Friday Viola and Rhelma came—Rhelma to stay over the week-end; Viola to live. How different it was from the home-coming which I had planned. All along, Viola had had doubts about the crazy venture—doubts which I was to share a hundred times, but the little mother of Goblin Wood, who had many a time carried her young baby on the pommel of her saddle seven miles up the old Stockyard Creek track, was not easily put aside by doubts. So Viola packed her things and headed for Lost World: bringing her savings which were added to my little roll. By this time, Rhelma, who had had business training, was earning her living in Brisbane. I had hoped to have a cosy room fixed up for Viola—something to take away a little of the raw newness of things—but most of all I wanted the glass corner windows looking out and up to the great crag of Mt. Widgee. Well, Viola would be able to see Widgee all right—there weren't even walls at that corner as yet, and the area where the beginnings of a garden and lawn had been planned was tangled vining Kikuyu grass, feet deep.

The river crossing was still out. Sam's taxi, which brought the ladies, used a private road which ended a mile away on the wrong side of the river. All of the gear we could manage we carried by hand and in the melancholy pre-dusk we waded through receding floodwaters fifty yards wide. One wonders what Viola's thoughts were as she forded the noisy torrent with its slippery boulders of rounded lava; what they were I've never asked. In the green singing dusk we came to the building. Balloon cicadas were droning in the cedars and fireflies winking in the gloom as we lit our lantern and got the stove going. The philosopher who said, "Home is where the heart is," might have added that it is usually where the stove is. A hot meal and then literally piles of new bedding. The next thing we knew it was dawn over Lost World and the butcher-birds were singing. There came a sound that was even more welcome—that of a heavy truck buzzing its way up the flats. Archie Stephens had "sooled" the Shire Council men on to the river crossing on the previous afternoon: and the red truck which had been so anti-Lost World at the outset of the venture, now decided to get with us and stoutly crossed the river, head-lights awash.

With the hammers and saws going merrily everyone's morale rose. For once the echoing hammer blows brought no reaction from the sky—at least not yet. Around noon the house had its first visitor—nephew Pete O'Reilly from Green Mountains, who had walked and climbed down—barefoot—by way of Castle Crag. Over Peter's shoulder was a bag which we thought might have contained his lunch, but which in fact contained an unusually large death adder. True, when Peter had started out he had lunch for himself and a large pineapple for us in the bag, but on a narrow ledge down Castle Crag, Peter put his big bare foot almost on top of the adder, as it slept coiled in the kangaroo grass. It was such a fine specimen that Peter decided to take it home and to this end he dumped the contents of the bag in the grass. The pineapple got a sudden roll on, leapt the cliff and was seen no more; that left the lunch and the adder and since they were ill-assorted Peter bagged the adder and ate the lunch. One had a feeling that a flip of a coin might have reversed the order. After a couple of hours Peter left for home and we watched him go, adder in bag, striding away up the ridges.

By the close of the week-end the structural work was about complete, but apart from one set of glass doors leading into the main room all doors and windows had yet to be fitted; there were no steps and no toilet. For this I had acquired a second-hand sentry-box type. Keith was to bring it out, but since it was heavy hardwood and in one piece he thought it wise to postpone operations until the river was lower. In any case Keith was to come out on Wednesday morning early with a team of men to finish everything off. With these assurances he drove off in the dusk, but before the sound of his truck had died away there was a rattle at the double-glass door: we had yet another visitor—it was that lady again. There was no red carpet out for the return of Bertha. The stony-hearted Victorian father who turned his erring daughter out into the storm was a soft sentimentalist compared with me and my feelings towards my lady visitor. The main trouble was that I was the one who was likely to be turned out into the storm.

Things could have been a great deal worse—this was to be a side-swipe off Point Danger. Bertha did not cross the coast a second time, but since such storms are often a thousand miles across they make things difficult within five hundred miles of the centre. On that Sunday night the wind rose to high velocity, but no rain fell until morning and then mainly as fairly heavy showers. We were still hoping for the best when at 3 p.m. "even time" rain set in again. There was a rush to get Rhelma away and across the river before high water came.

Bob Stephens drove his big Dodge up the private road on the far side of the river to pick Rhelma up and whisk her off down river in time to catch Peter Johnston's mail truck, which got out to Kerry before the bridges went under.

"There goes Easter!" Viola and I gasped as we fought our way home up the water-logged flats in the face of the wind and the rain. But Bertha, the eternal feminine, was unpredictable to the end; with the bridges under water and the river crossing scoured out she suddenly wheeled, marched out across the Tasman Sea and out of our lives.

It was of small consolation that the stars came out before bedtime and that Tuesday dawned in dazzling brightness. On Thursday evening, fifty-eight hours away, our guests were due and there were as yet no doors, no windows, no steps, no toilet, no food, no anything. Just a river that couldn't be crossed. Obviously the sensible thing to do would be to cancel the whole Easter operation—but had I specialized in doing the sensible thing I wouldn't have been at Lost World anyhow. Besides, the whole thing had become a glorious game, fought out round by round with the rain, the river and the wind; now, with the last round coming up, I wasn't going to throw in the towel.

I went on building in the double-decker beds, Viola was busy unpacking and sorting endless cases, cartons and bedrolls. In between times we'd go down and watch the river which was falling with painful slowness. It was worth watching anyhow—transparent blue-green and white, roaring, tumbling and joyful. Along the edges where the eddies had built small beaches of gravel wash, there glittered lovely rock crystals from water white to cloudy blue, which had been released from their cavities in the lava as the rocks split open in the torrent.

There were other stones, too—torn loose where the flood had undercut ancient sedimentary rock—stones with layer upon layer of fossil ferns as delicate and as beautiful in outline as the day they grew, back in the Jurassic period sixty million years ago. We thought as we looked at them: what would the next sixty million years bring? These mountains which towered from our feet would long have ceased to exist and their dust and rubble added to the sedimentary beds of the future and our trees and our plants buried in their spoil as the fossils of to-morrow. Would there still be scientists on earth to evaluate the record of the rocks, or would man, who even now was wearing out his welcome on earth, have vanished along with the mighty mountains which now look so permanent. Somehow as we looked at those fossils it didn't seem to matter a great deal whether the river went down, or the house got finished, or the Easter guests came.

On Wednesday great soft white clouds towered above the green border range; briefly the mountains whitened with rain, then clouds and rain dissolved into sunshine. This, typical of mid-autumn high-pressure systems, was nothing to cause alarm. It is normally a period of cool, fresh winds, bright sunshine and an occasional shower —glorious weather with nothing to fear by way of flood rain; but coming when the river was full and the earth running at its pores those showers would be just enough to slow the falling of the river. What now? Go on with it of course—long since it had been decided that there was to be no turning back.

Thursday morning and just twelve hours to go. I stripped off and swam in the fossil pool and came out feeling as though the world were mine. Of course we could manage even if the carpenters couldn't return; we would cleat the windows in temporarily and if necessary hang drapes for doors. Forty yards up the hill was a tall, hollow tree-stump part open on one side. I went up there after breakfast and began the task of outfitting the hollow stump as a toilet which would have been the joy of Chic Sale. From a purely artistic standpoint it is a pity that the project was never finished. It had only fairly got under way when, with the sound of a bomber taking off, the incredible red truck came around the bend, three carpenters jammed in the cabin and the toilet—complete—jammed in the back. Once more the Shire Council men had cleared the ford of rocks and the big truck had been part-coaxed and part-pushed through. That meant something else, too—by evening Graham's Chevvy truck would be able to lift our passengers and stores across the river and up to Lost World. It was in the bag!

Keith and his men swarmed over the house, fitting in doors and windows. Viola, making up beds in a room, found herself a prisoner as the door was nailed into place preparatory to hanging. She escaped to a second room only to have a second door nailed up across her way of retreat. The toilet was put over by the fence; it looked as though it had stood there all its life. However, the clock had one victim: time ran out before the steps could be made. Instead a ramp of square hard-wood gave access to the main room—it was safe and effective but very ugly.

At dusk I went across the river below the pumphouse and joined Graham and his brother Bruce in their truck, for the run down to the road crossing. Presently headlights came up the laneway—Lloyd's truck, and our precious Easter supplies. We offloaded and reloaded them on to the Chevvy.

There were a few minutes to wait before our guests were due—and those few minutes brought disquietening reflections. In the maze of difficulties which had beset us there had been little time to speculate about our coming guests and their reactions to our wild new valley and our raw new building. In a normal time we could have taken people to the house in the comfort of a car—now they would have to travel the final two miles on a table-top truck, exposed to any weather that might come. As though to give point to the latter a great black cloudbank advanced from the east, blocking out the valley and the mountains and the rising moon. A wild rainsquall hosed us down just as the headlights of our guests' car appeared around the bend half-a-mile away, but mountain weather with superb showmanship was about to put on one of its finest acts. As the car came to a stop on the riverbank the clouds were split wide as by a silver sword, they rolled back in fleeces of white across the black mountains, a great round Easter moon rode on the lip of Mt. Worendo and the wild silver river ran for joy. That moment of magic set the mood of the holiday; there was merriment in the mounting of the truck, adventure in the wheel-deep crossing of the river, and every bump along the road was greeted by laughter and comment and cheers.

That night, too, set the weather pattern of the holiday; an odd shower, dazzling sunshine, roaring white water, dripping rainforest, and mountains playing hide and seek in the clouds. Late on Easter Monday when Graham came again with the Chevvy we rode with our new friends down across the river to wave them off in their car. Walking home we were thoroughly drenched. It was the last of the showers—Easter was over.

Epilogue

SLOWLY and sometimes painfully we dug in our toes at Lost World: bit by bit we enlarged and improved the place—an addition here, a new building there. The ramp gave way to a long concrete patio: the storied toilet was replaced by septics and electric light took the place of our pressure lamps. Then, happy day, a new dining-room with many windows looking up into the big wild country.

The weather, once it found that it couldn't lick us, gave up and came around to our side. Apart from a big flood in February 1956 and a playful cyclone in 1959—which picked up the dining-room roof and dumped it a few hundred yards away—the elements have been quite tame.

Rhelma took an office job in Beaudesert and lived with us at Lost World—driving her Holden twenty-five miles each way daily . . . sometimes headlight-deep through the river. But the river is a friendly river now and rarely throws its weight about. The wild days will return when the weather cycle makes its full turn—just now we are enjoying the days of peace but with a tingle of excitement for the days to come when the big wild fellows come spinning once more out of the Coral Sea and the river again lifts its white mane with a roar of anger.

As a business venture Lost World has not been a great success. Probably the fault was mine in misjudging the temper of modern youth. It is a little sad to think that many people have lost their sense of daring—that they cling to the easy and the well-trodden ways while the vast wilderness calls with the thrilling voice of adventure and a new world lies beyond each range.

But Lost World was not a failure—in peace, tranquillity and family happiness it has brought riches beyond reckoning and to our little Rhelma it has brought romance: even as the last words of this book were written—in the spring of 1960 Rhelma became Mrs. Barry Kenny.

Postscript 1963

AS this book goes to press our Lost World adventure has run its full cycle; a good adventure it has been and a light-hearted one, but behind it all was the serious business of re-learning the art of living, for unless we learn to come to terms with life we remain as strangers in a foreign element.

The sadness we feel in leaving our valley will be offset by the fact that we are returning to our old love "Goblin Wood." There will be busy and exciting days ahead in the rescuing of "Goblin Wood" from the green fingers of the forest, in rebuilding it and planning a wilder garden than before. The satin brigands will be waiting for us— there is a well-stocked bower twenty-yards from the back door; the little people of the rainforest, who have been my friends since 1917, will all be there to see to it that we do not sleep late of mornings nor lack company through the day. There will be no vain regrets for the pains and the plannings that went into our valley buildings. The

important things built in that valley are the ones
we shall be taking with us.

                                BERNARD O'REILLY.
August 1963.